AL-KIMIA

THE MYSTICAL ISLAMIC ESSENCE
OF THE SACRED ART OF ALCHEMY

JOHN EBERLY

AL-KIMIA

THE MYSTICAL
ISLAMIC ESSENCE
OF THE SACRED ART
OF ALCHEMY

SOPHIA PERENNIS

HILLSDALE NY

First published in the USA
by Sophia Perennis
© copyright 2004

Series editor: James R. Wetmore

For information, address:
Sophia Perennis, P.O. Box 611
Hillsdale NY 12529
sophiaperennis.com

Printed in the
United States of America

Library of Congress Cataloging-in-Publication Data

Eberly, John.
Al-Kimia: the mystical essence of the sacred art of alchemy /
John Eberly.—1st ed.

p. cm.

Includes bibliographical references.
ISBN 0 900588 48 9 (pbk: alk. paper)
1. Alchemy—Islamic Empire,—History.
2. Sufis—Arab countries—Biography. I. Title.
QD 18.1742 E23 2004
540'.1'12—dc22   2004019337

DEDICATED IN LOVING MEMORY
TO NANCY ANNE EBERLY GOFF (1938–1995),
WHO NEVER STOPPED BELIEVING IN HER BROTHER

ACKNOWLEDGEMENTS

THE AUTHOR wishes to thank: the Holy Wisdom in which all is accomplished; James Wetmore for his vision; Lynnette Krehbiel for pouring over the manuscript, correcting it, and making many valuable suggestions; Paul Green for his reading of the manuscript in preparation; Naomi Stiggins for her trust and love; Paul Hawkins, Jim and Lisa French, Merida Blanco, Gaylord Dold, and Gene Grier for their understanding and support; Charles Upton for his tenacity, Mr. Mashallah Niktab for his sublime station, all my fellow darvishes and alchemists for their perseverance, my beloved family, and to the Master for everything, *apha et omega*, all thanks to you. *Per Nos omnia.* Ya Haqq!

ABOUT THE TEXT

IN THE FOLLOWING WORK, Arabic and Persian transliterations abound. Great care has been taken to place the English equivalent definition of such terms adjacent to their transliterated appearance in the text, for example: *qalb* or heart. However, if this care has somehow been neglected or if the reader is not satisfied with the abbreviated definitions, reference should be made to the Glossary, an abridgement of the author's previous work: *A Glossary of Transliterated Islamic Sufi Terms and Phrases* (Wichita: Anamnesis Press, 1992), born from a similar frustration in reading texts which rely on copious transliterations of terms.

Kem is considered to be the original Arabic name for Egypt or Nubia, which roughly means black or fertile earth. Any term that relates to this original Arabic name for the place that produced the sacred art of metallurgy and considered gold to be the spiritual essence of the Sun and silver to be the spiritual essence of the Moon etymologically finds its source at the valley of the Nile. Such terms as the Arabic *al-Kimia*, also spelled *Alchimia,* and more commonly westernized as *Alchemy,* and the variations of usage (alchemist, alchemical, etc.), are used interchangeably in the following text, and refer back to the root *Kem.* Perhaps by intuition the reader can also follow this seemingly backward progression into the present tense.

Care has also been taken to explain by footnotes, in addition to the text, the origin of source material. When explanation has been omitted, the reader may assume that the source is non-specific. For example, while several different translations of the Qur'an were used, supplying specific translation notes for each quotation seemed unwarranted. Certain traditions and legends are often undocumented, and have at times been reduced to their basic information in order to keep the text concise. If a topic which requires the use of notation is not explained to the reader's satisfaction, reference should be made to the Bibliography, which may occasionally duplicate source entries found originally in the footnotes and vice versa.

A word of caution may be in order for the reader who is encountering any of these subjects for the first time. For example, alchemical texts generally make use of repetition of key words or phrases. Repetition of these words and phrases may eventually become absorbed and assimilated within the consciousness of the reader and be understood in subtle ways that words linearly and in their degenerative literal presentation cannot be comprehended. It is also helpful to remember that Sufism, Shi'ism, Ismailism, Art, and al-Kimia all utilize terminologies and vocabularies specific to their respective disciplines. Often a common definition of a term is not only insufficient but also misleading.

'Wine', when associated with Sufism, is a term symbolizing a tangible spiritual substance most often (but not always, please refer to the Glossary) conceived of in a poetic, allegorical sense. Many have been led astray by assigning literal meanings to the terms 'mercury', 'sulphur', and 'salt', commonly found in the texts of al-Kimia. On occasion, alchemical writers preface these terms with the word 'philosophic' so that the would-be student will not become discouraged.

These are not, it is hoped, impassable hurdles in the examination of this text. Initial familiarization of terms is required in the study of almost any new subject. The author has made every attempt to approach the material presented with an appreciation of its difficulty and has hopefully rendered what is offered with some degree of general comprehensibility.

CONTENTS

PREFACE

He is the First, and the Last, and the Outward and the Inward; and He is the knower of all things.

QUR'AN (57:3)

Wither shall I look when I praise Thee? Upward or downward, inward or outward? For Thou art the place in which all things are contained: there is no other place beside Thee: all things are in thee.'

HERMES TRISMEGISTOS

THE FIRST MATTER, the *prima materia* of any alchemical operation undertaken, must begin with idea. The main idea for this short work is found in *stone* in Eran-Vej on Mount Hukairya, where the wondrous *Haoma* tree of eternal life grows. From this artful tree the Elixir of Immortality is made. Nearby grows another tree which cures all ills and contains within itself the seeds of all plants. Close to Hukairya stands a mountain of ruby, the first earth to receive the dawn, the transmutation, or the *dawning of intelligence*.

In order to approach the subject *matter* engendered by the title of this book one must be ready to exercise at will the area of perception which Henry Corbin called the *imaginal*,[1] and agree that, in this context, symbol is not mere metaphor but is identified so closely with that which is symbolized as to render subject and object *essentially* inseparable.

This work is about experiencing the world through a body of flesh mingled with spirit in which the drama of experience exists most

---

1. See: Henry Corbin, *Creative Imagination in the Sufism of Ibn 'Arabi*; Prologue to Part Two, 'Creative Imagination and Creative Prayer', pp179–183. This brief prologue provides only a glimpse of the concept of the *imaginal* which is, of course, grasped more thoroughly by a close reading of the entire work.

palpably in the heart and not foremost in the mind. It is the work of Nature in which everything experientially and intuitively participates. At its best, the text attempts to leap beyond the merely conceptual into the Void of unknowing. If it falls short of the mark, may it then simply serve to uncover the topsoil of a vast and deep garden of mysteries.

Herein are found certain special people, all of whom are related by their association with an occult art, which represents a way of living that transcends religious dogma without causing it violence, while simultaneously adapting to prismatic social and cultural considerations. Because of the selfless acts of the examined adepts of this art, existence is more bearable, more enjoyable, and far more interesting. Anyone with an interest in Alchemy, Sufism, and Islam, or Hermeticism in general, may be familiar with some of the people discussed, including: al-Hallaj, Ibn 'Arabi, al-'Iraqi, and Bayazid al-Bistami. With the notable exception of Ibn 'Arabi, who potentially represents a pivot upon which the whole revolves, the people in this group are really mentioned in passing. Their lives and contributions have been well documented elsewhere. The Bibliography provides a listing of excellent reference works such as the four volume *The Passion of al-Hallaj*, the life's work of the great Louis Massignon; or the more modest, yet also wonderful, *Quest for the Red Sulphur: The Life of Ibn 'Arabi*, by Claude Addas, daughter of Michel Chodkiewitz, an author whose work is also often quoted in the following study.

This brief examination will also survey the lives and thought of some who are perhaps not as well known in the West as those mentioned above, yet all are certainly deserving of closer attention. The common thread throughout is al-Kimia, and it must be noted that the lives of certain alchemists often resemble or are in fact the lives of saints. Perhaps the unverifiable facts concerning these alchemists may be more deserving of a title such as *The Golden Legend*.

The term Alchemy is so overused that it is nearly devoid of meaning, and yet most who use it often apply it within a correct context, despite the fact that when pressed for a precise definition, the honest will balk. Generally considered, the term Alchemy tends to conjure up the mysterious. In the Islamic world at least, Alchemy signifies *process* and the summation of a process, and is identified with the term process to such an extent that we are often confronted with, 'The Alchemy of (This)' or 'The Alchemy of (That)'. For example, an early Muslim ascetic, Shaqiq al-Balkhi, formulated what he called the 'Alchemy of Hunger', in which he claimed that forty days of constant hunger would transform the darkness of the heart into light.

Seyyed Hossein Nasr, in his classic work *Sufi Essays*, sums up al-Kimia thus:

> Alchemy, which is at once a symbolic science of material forms and a symbolic expression of the spiritual and psychological transformations of the soul, became a link between Sufism and art, and its language the means whereby the maker and the artisan has been given the possibility of integrating his outward and inward life, his work and his religious activity.[2]

To describe this little book as simply a hagiography of Islamic alchemists is perhaps not adequate. It also attempts to present the reader with a broader definition of other related subjects.

This is not, however, a study based on dissection and specialization. It purports to be about something whole and unified. In true alchemical fashion this amounts to the famous maxim: *Solve et coagula, et habebis magisterium* (Dissolve and bind, and you will have the masterpiece). One must dissolve the parts and recombine them with their essence in the crucible of Unity so that a real understanding of the work might *project* upon the blank canvas of the reader's *prima materia*.

> From this myriad multiplicity we have emerged through the grace of the Friend into the realm of the Universal.[3]

DR. JAVAD NURBAKHSH

Muhammad is a man, not like other men, but like a precious *stone* among *stones*.

ALI IBN ABI TALIB

---

2. *Sufi Essays* (Albany: SUNY Press, 1972), p 48.

3. Nurbakhsh, Javad, *The Truths of Love* (New York: Khaniqahi-Nimatullahi, 1982), from #22.

INTRODUCTION

There is no thing whose treasuries are not with Us.

QU'RAN (15:21)

THE ART OF AL-KIMIA is the *summa*, the perfection of sages, the prophets, the saints; it is the goal and process of the famous Hermetic phrase *'as above, so below.'* This sacred art has no purpose outside the precepts of Nature's laws. The alchemist is aware that all creation is solely dependent upon the Creator and that nothing is achieved outside of the will of God. He understands, rather, that his work, indeed his very existence, *is* the will of God. al-Kimia accelerates the natural evolutionary process in order to accomplish, *insh'Allah*, the spiritualization of matter and the materialization of the Holy Spirit. The Qur'an reveals this necessary relationship between God and man,

We are nearer to him than the jugular vein.

QUR'AN (50:16)

The human is the intermediate locus where potential comes into being, is actuated by becoming, and witnesses the spiritual as result. It is also the place where the spiritual comes into being, is actuated, and witnesses *being* as result. As below, so above.

According to the *Stobaei Hermetica*, in the section 'Exc. XXIII (Kore Kosmu)' in which the Egyptian goddess Isis speaks to her son Horus,

But when he [God] determined to reveal himself, he breathed into certain godlike men a passionate desire to know him, and bestowed on their minds a radiance ampler than that which they already had in their breasts, that so they might first will to seek the yet unknown God, and then have the power to find him. But this, Horus my wondrous son, it would not have been possible for men of mortal breed to do, if there had not arisen one whose soul was responsive to the influence of the holy Powers of heaven. Such a man was Hermes, he who won knowledge of all. Hermes saw all things, and understood what he saw, and had power to explain to others what he understood ... for what he had discovered he inscribed on tablets, and hid securely what he had inscribed, leaving the larger part untold, that all later ages of the world may seek it.

Separation, a term common to a process in al-Kimia, may be an essential *concept* that engenders the yearning of the *part* for the *whole*.

A principal figure in al-Kimia, whether historical or legendary, is Hermes Trismegistos or Thrice Great Hermes, who is identified with the Qur'anic (19:56–57, 21:85) prophet Idris in the Islamic world. Like three other Qur'anic prophets, Khezr, Elijah, and Jesus, Hermes is believed to have been carried off alive by God at the proposed time of death. The earliest translation in Arabic of 'The Emerald Tablet,' by Hermes Trismegistos, reproduced in Appendix II, is attributed to Jabir Ibn Hayyan. In 'The Emerald Tablet' is found the origin of the famous unitarian phrase used so liberally in al-Kimia, '*as above, so below.*'

The Qur'an is the God-revealed text to the Arabic people in their native language. It shares its point of origin with the revealed texts of the Hebrews, and the Christians, both of whom the Qur'an identifies as 'people of the book'.

The sacred relationship between God and his revealed word congealed in the form of the text is an essential aspect of al-Kimia as well. In ancient Egypt, Tehuti, or Thoth-Hermes (Trismegistos) is depicted hieroglyphically as an Ibis-headed *scribe* who wears the symbols of creation on his head. The Ibis-head symbolizes the alchemist's vessel of distillation known as the *retort*. Alchemical texts often speak of reading the Great Book of Nature. To the Adept, Nature is an 'open book' simple in style and easy to read providing one can decipher it: this turns out to be the difficult part of the process. Sendivogius[1] calls the prepared mercury of the philosophic *stone* a 'flakey' mass in which the crystalline layers lie one on top of the other like the *leaves of a book*, which is indeed open to those who can read it, and closed to others.

Certainly the book was opened for the Islamic alchemists who are examined in the following text. Some of these alchemists were also Sufi saints and mystics who found inspiration, *Nafas ar-Rahman*, the holy breath of the Merciful, in the revelation of the holy book of Islam, al-Qur'an. In almost every chapter in the following text we find that the alchemists have left us, 'the later ages of the world,' with numerous texts, which like Hermes, the father of Hermetica and al-Kimia, 'inscribed, leaving the larger part untold.'

R.A. Schwaller de Lubicz, a twentieth-century adept of al-Kimia has been quoted on the importance of this aspect of our subject,

> It's obscurity [the text] ... can evaporate in an instant, the instant the reader discovers the author's mentality, his bias, his angle of vision. With a good author, the discovery can be akin to a revelation, an opening of perception, and that is the value of the text. I could give you a version of this text that explains every image, every analogy, every mythological or astrological reference and correspondence, and you would have learned nothing. It is not a learning you are after, it is a God-given revelation which is hindered by any rational interference. I would be destroying the text if I wrote a glossary.

As we have noted above, and so it is here again applicable below, al-Kimia's roots in written text literally begin with the first stories of creation, which remain inexplicable to the veiled perception.

The Qu'ranic prophet Khezr, previously mentioned in relation to Hermes Trismegistos, is identified with Alexander the Great's cook, Andreas, who accompanied him on his search for the spring of eternal life. Andreas, who finds the spring and drinks of it to become the immortal Khezr, represents the aspect of humanity that values the spirit. Alexander, as the temporal king of the material

---

1. Michael Sendivogius, b. 1566 in Moravia, d. 1646 in Parma. Author of a collection of alchemical treatises entitled *A New Light on Alchemy*.

world, symbolizes the vain human quest for fame and fortune. This story echoes the sentiments of adepts of all ages who assert that the goal of al-Kimia, which has erroneously been held to be solely the manufacture of gold, has never been achieved for material gain nor for power in a personal material context.

Beyond its traceable origin in ancient *Kem*, the essence of al-Kimia *coalesced* in the fourth century BC multicultural climate of the Egyptian city of Alexandria, a meeting place for various philosophical, scientific, and spiritual teachings.

During the siege of Alexandria perpetrated by Julius Caesar in 47 BC, fire destroyed part of the first and most famous universal library housing a collection in excess of 400,000 *rotuli* or scrolls, including original written alchemical lore. Much of this knowledge, however, had already passed into Greek culture and was transmitted to Arabia with the spread of Islam.

The presentation of this text is potentially in microcosm representative of the macrocosm of esoteric Islamic Alchemy, a living tradition existing in eternity within the primordial unborn spiritual condition of humanity in which God asks the heart's atoms,

Am I not your Lord (To which they reply): 'Yes!'

QUR'AN (7:172)

I

THE ARC OF ASCENT

1

KHALID IBN YAZID

ONE OF THE FIRST ARAB RECIPIENTS of al-Kimia was Khalid ibn Yazid (c. 665–704). Khalid is credited as being a link between the Alexandrian and the subsequent Arabian schools of al-Kimia.

Khalid ibn Yazid was the grandson of Muawiya, founder of the Umayyad dynasty.[1] According to tradition, by age twenty Khalid left Damascus for Alexandria, where he met his teacher or teachers, Stephanus the Elder and his protégé Morienus, a hermit of Jerusalem. A story concerning the fateful meeting of student and teacher begins one day when Prince Khalid mysteriously acquired a text containing the secrets of the Philosopher's Stone. Unable to fathom the contents of the work, he offered a generous reward to anyone who might be able to decipher the text's secrets. False alchemists and tricksters flocked to his court to waste his time and money without succeeding to produce an interpretation. The Christian hermit Morienus, upon hearing about the prince and the mysterious text, set off to visit him. In a short time Morienus was able to demonstrate how the text might be used to produce the Philosopher's Stone. Khalid was very pleased with the result, and ordered the execution of all the alchemical pretenders. Morienus apparently vanished back into the desert only to reappear later to further instruct his new pupil. By all accounts, Khalid ibn Yazid continued on to become a good Umayyad Caliph, a preacher, a poet, and a wise and articulate man.

In the Arabian encyclopedia (c. 985) by Ibn al-Nadim titled *Kitab al-Fihrist*, the following three alchemical verses are attributed to Khalid:

1. For more on the Umayyads see *A History of Islamic Societies*, Ira M. Lapidus (NY: Cambridge Univ. Press, 1988), pp 56–67, and generally throughout the book.

Take talc with ammonia and what is found in the street; take a substance that resembles borax and pulverize everything without committing an error; then, if you love God your lord, you shall be Nature's master.[1]

In the brief tract: *The Book Of Knowledge Acquired Concerning The Cultivation of Gold: An Arabic Alchemical Treatise*, by al-'Iraqi, there appears a conversation between Khalid the pupil and Morienus the master. The content, in the form of question and answer, concludes with the following:

[Khalid said] is the operation now finished, or does anything still remain of which thou hast not told me? [He-Morienus, said] it is finished for him who likes brevity, but as for him who wishes to continue, let him moisten the substance of Everlasting Water which he has already prepared, and it will increase in tinctorial power endlessly, and will absorb all the liquid with which he moistens it, to infinity.' Khalid marveled at this.[2]

In Step 8 under the chapter heading 'The Herbal Elixir' in his *Alchemist's Handbook*, Frater Albertus (d. 1984) instructs:

The potency of this elixir may be increased by calcining it in a calcining dish. This is returned to the flask of the extraction apparatus, and the circulation is repeated with more of the extracted essence. Each time this is done, the potency will be increased.[3]

Frater then adds yet another step which produces a *stone*. It follows from this comparison that the alchemical process essentially remains the same, whether the alchemist is working in the vegetable, animal, or mineral kingdom, each of which, of course, must be dealt with separately.

1. *The Fihrist of al-Nadim*, edited and translated by Bayard Dodge, 2 vols (New York: Columbia Univ. Press, 1970).

2. Al-Iraqi, *The Book of Knowledge Acquired Concerning the Cultivation of Gold: An Arabic Treatise* (Edmonds, WA: The Alchemical Press, 1991), p47.

3. Albertus, Frater, *Alchemist's Handbook* (New York: Weiser, 1960), p35.

According to Ibn al-Nadim, Khalid authored several books and a series of alchemical poems on the art, including *The Book of Amulets, The Great and Small Books of the Scroll, The Paradise of Wisdom,* and *Legacy to My Son About the Art.* This last title is in all likelihood the work of the Imam Jafar as-Sadiq (see next chapter).

The story of the life and work of the alchemist Khalid Ibn Yazid illustrates the importance of two prime factors often involved in accessing the art of al-Kimia: the text and the teacher. Khalid's introduction to the mysterious text which he could not decipher, and the indispensable aid of Morienus, is echoed by the story of the four-teenth-century French alchemist Nicholas Flamel. Flamel came into the possession of a text entitled *The Book of Abraham the Jew.* He recognized it as a work of value containing material far beyond his comprehension. After several false starts on his own initiative and a dubious interpretation by a man who claimed to be deeply interested in Alchemy, Flamel finally set out on a pilgrimage and found a certain Master Canches. Master Canches initiated Flamel into the art of al-Kimia by a Qabalistic interpretation of the text, thereby producing the Philosopher's Stone.[4]

The transmission of occult knowledge passing between master and disciple is a recurring aspect of initiation in mystical schools. This transmission often relies upon the appearance or legacy of textual material.

4. The story of Nicholas Flamel is legendary alchemical lore. It is found in nearly every history of Alchemy. For a good accounting of the tale see *Alchemy Rediscovered and Restored,* by Archibald Cockren, (Philadelphia: David McKay, 1940),pp30–39.

2

JAFAR AS-SADIQ

THE IDEA OF THE IMAM in Shi'a Islam as the pole of the universe is closely related to the Sufi concept of the perfect master or *qutb*. In fact, the two are nearly identical and refer to the same essential Islamic reality, the *haqiqat al-muhammadiyyah*. It is rare, however, that both Shi'a Imam and Sufi *qutb* come together in one person after 'Ali, the patron saint of Sufism and first Imam of Shi'a Islam. This was indeed the case with the unique Imam and *qutb*, Jafar as-Sadiq.

Jafar was the sixth 'Alid Imam who appears as a central figure in Shi'a, Sufi, and Ismaili *silsilas* or initiatory chains. He was a prolific writer who founded the *Jafari*, the Twelve Imam Shi'ite school of law which engendered the Twelve Imam Shi'ites (Twelvers or *ithna 'ashariyyah*),[1] and wrote commentaries on al-Qu'ran which include the concept of *jafr*, a way to interpret layered meanings of key verses that disclose prophecy and revelation through the numerical value assigned to the letters of the alphabet. In response to a question concerning the perpetual freshness of the revelation found in al-Qu'ran -a concept that Ibn 'Arabi would expand upon later by explaining that revelation is only revelation when it alights anew upon the heart of the reciter *in the act of recitation*, Jafar said:

> [It is] because the Qu'ran is not for an exclusive age or for an exclusive people.[2]

---

1. For more on Twelvers, Ismailis, and Shi'ites in general, see the present work, chapter seven, 'Ismailis, Sufis, and al-Kimia.'
2. *Shi'ism: Doctrines, Thought, and Spirituality,* edited by S.H. Nasr, et.al., (Albany: SUNY, 1988), p33.

Jafr likely had its origin in Greek Gnosticism and certainly shares similarities with exegetical systems found within the Hebrew Qabala. Sufism and Shi'a share a process of hermeneutic interpretation known as *ta'wil*, which is in a broader sense much like *jafr*. Jafar al-Sadiq also stated:

> The angels are peripheral, knowing only some of God's Names, while man is central, knowing all His Names.[3]

According to the mystic, Shibli (Abu Bakr Dolaf Ja'far ibn Yunos al-Shebli, d. 846), a contemporary of al-Hallaj:

> When God created the letters, he kept their secrets for Himself, and when he created Adam, He conveyed this secret to him, but did not convey it to any of His angels.[4]

This central position afforded only to the perfected human being is echoed in another saying of Jafar's:

> In this world, the life of the Imam and the life of the Holy Book are bound together.[5]

All systems of interpreting holy books (and indeed, all of creation) find common ground with al-Kimia, which not only sees in the same texts prescriptions of the *art* but also claims that this is the real exegetical interpretation to be uncovered and understood.

Frater Albertus explained it thus:

> If, by divine wisdom, man, as highest specimen of the animal realm, has been placed in the middle of the three kingdoms (vegetable, animal, mineral), it has been of necessity, since nothing in Nature is based on chance. Man is holding the balance of the three kingdoms and can partake of any one according to his liking, having an alchemical laboratory in his own body to

3. Ad-Hadith, not traced.
4. See Annemarie Schimmel's *Mystical Dimensions of Islam* (Chapel Hill: Univ. of North Carolina Press, 1975), p412, quoting from Gustav Flugel, *Die arabischen, persischen und turkischen Handschriften in der K.K. Hofbibliothek zu Wien* (Vienna, 1865–67), 1:192.
5. *Shi'ism*: p178.

transmute inorganic matter into organic, and organic into spiritual matter.'[6]

Al-Kimia is famous for arcane alphabets, symbology, and seemingly impenetrable texts. In this way it shares a sense of self-preservation with Hermeticism in general and specifically with other often endangered 'heresies' such as Shi'ite Islam, which employs its own survival tactic in the practice of *taqiyyah*, roughly translated as: concealment.

Jafar the Imam and the *qutb* was also Jafar the alchemist. Several alchemical tracts apparently penned using the pseudonym 'al-Hakim' are attributed to him including a letter of protection which lists the following prescription for obtaining the Elixir of Life, the Great Red Water:

1. Calcination. 2. Treatment of the Spirit. 3. 'Bleaching' the Soul. 4. Uniting Body, Spirit, and Soul by means of the Great Red Water. 5. Fixing the 'Little Elixir'. 6. Projecting the Elixir. 7. The Great Red Water comes into Being.[7]

Two of his other alchemical titles include the *Book of Jafar as-Sadiq's Message Concerning the Science of the Art and the Precious Stone*, and the *Copy of the Tawhid of al-Hakim, Ruler of Egypt, Concerning the Science of the Noble Art*.

Imam Jafar as-Sadiq was a *qutb* of immense insight into the Mysteries. It is estimated that he had over four thousand students, both Sunni and Shi'a. More *ad-Hadith* or traditions have come down to us from him than from all other Imams put together. He said,

The intelligence is that through which man worships the All-Merciful and gains Paradises.[8]

Many Sufi concepts can be traced directly to this sublime teacher. One is the following basic definition of Divine Love often repeated by later mystics:

6. *Alchemist's Handbook* (see chap. 1, n 4), p 30.
7. *Tawhid of al-Hakim*, not traced.
8. *A Shi'ite Anthology*, edited by William C. Chittick (Albany: SUNY, 1981), p 55.

[Love is] a Divine Fire that devours man completely.[9]

This is both a concise and apt description of spiritual alchemical calcination.

It should be apparent now that the concept of al-Kimia works simultaneously on several levels of awareness. It may seem as if we are talking about a purely physical or philosophical phenomena when in truth this is a point where exoteric and esoteric meet, compliment one another, and find union. The *qutb*, the Imam Jafar as-Sadiq had this to say concerning the complete and utter Unity of God or *Tawhid*,

> He does not terminate at a limit unless it be other than He...He is named by His names, so He is other than His names, and His names are other than He.[10]

Conception must comply with the same laws that Nature prescribes, *solve et coagula*, dissolve and coagulate.

> Concepts may give you transient rest, but what I offer is truly the peace which passeth all understanding.[11]

YAHYA ABD AT-TAWWAB

What Jafar has to say in a given context may most certainly apply in another (or any other) context. The same is true of mystics and alchemists who find themselves *at the center of Being*. This may also serve to illustrate an exceptional musician's universal appeal, a great poet's language of symbol and allegory, and a gifted painter's obvious depiction of an inner/outer reality.

In another Qur'anic commentary, Jafar formulated the psychological distinctions between the *nafs*, the lowest principle in man, *qalb*, the heart, and the *ruh*, or spirit; distinctions adopted by the Sufi community and later expounded by Bayazid Bistami, Tirmidhi, and Junayd among many, many other subsequent Sufi masters. He

9. *Mystical Dimensions of Islam*, p41, quoting from Paul Nwyia, S.J., *Exegese coranique et langage mystique*, Beirut, 1970.

10. *Shi'ism*: p122.

11. From the *Moqa'ta'at of Yahya Abd at-Tawwab* (manuscript).

also introduced the idea of *'aql* (reason) as the barrier between *nafs* and *qalb*. 'The barrier which they both cannot transcend' (Qur'an 227:20) has remained a basic Sufi teaching model.

The alchemist's Salt is a concept of the body, the indestructible aspect of created things always found at the earth's crust linking the vegetable, animal, and mineral kingdoms. Hence the phrase, 'he is the *salt* of the earth.' Sulphur is sometimes considered the Soul or intermediate part at the 'heart' of the matter, where is found the Sol, the Sun (Son) of God, the Eternal Flame. Mercury symbolizes the active Spirit. Only by the fire of Divine Love can the body and soul be reconciled within the spirit.

Can *reason* conceive of this process? Is there a *reason* for life or death? Can anyone think of a *reason* for an after-life, a resurrection? These questions cannot transcend the barrier they encounter without the intermediary attention of God's representatives, perfect masters like Jafar as-Sadiq who alchemically activate the 'peace which passeth all understanding.'

3

ABU MUSA
JABIR IBN HAYYAN

Alas! Till now I did not know that the alchemy of felicity means a
'good companion'!

HAFEZ

JAFAR'S FOUR THOUSAND STUDENTS included two famous
founders of Sunni law, Malik ibn Anas and Abu Hanifah, but one
student in particular stands out in the history of al-Kimia. His full
name is Abu Musa Jabir Ibn Hayyan; however, we know him simply
as Jabir, or, Geber. It is in this last transliterated form that the name
of the most famous of all Arabic-speaking alchemists survives, and
invariably this is the name most often found accompanying the few
works of his that remain. The continued use of the name Geber
attests to the importance of his writings for practitioners of
Alchemy in the West, who have found his often complicated systems to be of invaluable practical worth. It should be mentioned at
the outset that Jabir considered *all* of his work to be no more than
an account of his master Jafar's teachings.

For example, similar to his master's exegetical *jafr*, Jabir employed
a system ascribing alternate meanings to numbers and also to letters
of the alphabet. This system is not Qu'ranic *jafr*, however; there can
be no doubt that *jafr* is the influential antecedent and the point of
reference for comparison.

Jabir was born in Tus, a city in Khurasan, between 721 and 730 and
was a descendant of a south Arabian tribe. Some sources state that

he was not, in fact, a Muslim but a Harranian Sabian; however, this assertion is based on dubious information. He was an initiate into al-Kimia and also Sufism by association with his master Jafar. It has been noted how the spiritual and physical dimensions of the human may come together in this art, and indeed, as far as Jabir, the student of Sufism and al-Kimia is concerned, this fusion is essential:

No one can excel in the alchemical art without knowing the principles in himself; and the greater the knowledge of self, the greater will be the magnetic power attained thereby and the greater the wonders to be realized.[1]

CORNELIUS AGRIPPA, paraphrasing Jabir

Jabir was once court chemist to Harun al-Rashid, the Abbasid caliph; yet until his death somewhere between 810 and 815 he seems to have spent most of his life in Kufa, doing alchemical research.

In the *Fihrist*,[2] Jabir enumerates his vast corpus of written works:

I have written 300 works on philosophy, 1,300 books about the works of art (Ruska believes this phrase to refer to machines, automats, specific instructions, and the like), and 1,300 works on the combined subjects of arts and machinery of war. Also, I have written an extensive book on medicine, as well as other smaller and larger works, to a total of some 500 books on medicine, including the *Book on Diagnosis and Anatomy*. I also wrote books on logic, based on the views of Aristotle. Then I composed the sophisticated Astronomical Table of some 300 pages, the *Book of Euclidean Commentaries*, the *Commentaries to the Almagest* (the Ptolemaic astronomy), the *Book of Mirrors*, books on asceticism, horatory books, books on spells and exorcism ... and finally I wrote a book on the art (alchemistry) known as the *Book of the King*, and a book known as *The Gardens*.[3]

---

1. Julius Evola, *The Hermetic Tradition: Symbols and Teachings of the Royal Art* (Rochester: Inner Traditions, 1995), p 25.
2. *The Fihrist of al-Nadim*, op. cit.
3. Ibid.

The *Fihrist* goes on to list some 250 alchemical titles but specifically calls this the 'abridged' catalogue.

In one of his many works, Jabir cites the Greek philosophical pentads and the five Platonic bodies and cites as well the doctrine of Empedocles, who speaks of materia prima, intelligence, soul, nature, and corporeal matter. Jabir divides the created world into substance, matter, form, time, and space.

Jabir first proposed that the vegetable, animal, and mineral kingdoms were respectively fused or composed of the philosophic (as opposed to literal) sulphur and mercury. He saw that each kingdom evolved under planetary influences.

Jabir divides minerals into three groups: Spirits or substances which completely evaporate under heat; metals or fusible or malleable substances which shine or ring; and substances which fusible or not are not malleable but may be pulverized. According to Jabir, spirits are sulphur and the sulfuric compounds, while metals are seven; gold, silver, lead, tin, copper, iron, and something he called Chinese iron, which was probably a copper-zinc-nickel alloy.

The various metals exist, according to Jabir, because pristine (philosophic) sulphur and mercury rarely occur in a pure state. If this rarity occurs, the result is gold. Since all metals are composed of the same basic element, the transmutation of each metal into the other is possible by the intermediary of the Great Red Water, or Elixir of Jafar. This model possibly originated with his master or is an adaptation expanding upon the original. In either case, it was adopted by alchemists for centuries thereafter. The great ocean of influence generated first by the Sufi *qutb* and Shi'ite Imam Jafar and later articulated by his *murid* Jabir cannot be overestimated!

In his exegetical system, which takes, at the very least, a point of departure from *jafr*, Jabir assigns a number from one to twenty-eight for each of the twenty-eight letters of the Arabic alphabet. He also makes use of the magic square, already known to the Neoplatonists, which produces the number seventeen when the four numbers at the lower left corner of the square are added. These numbers are three, five, eight, and one. When these numbers are considered separately, three has multiple meanings bringing immediately to mind philosophical sulphur, mercury, and salt. Five, in relation to

Jabir, has already been discussed concerning his division of the created world. Seventeen is the number Jabir assigns to the various powers attributed to metals. Adding the one and the seven in seventeen we get eight, which symbolizes among other things, the Hermetic 'as above, so below.' One is so potent a symbol that it may pass without comment after 'say one, see one, be one.' It has been proposed that Jabir left the number nine out of his system because this number signifies completion, the final work, the Red Elixir. Adding the three, six (and zero) of the three hundred and sixty degrees of the circle totals nine, which is also the sum of the two Greek letters Alpha and Omega (one hundred and eight: one plus zero plus eight). The variations in this system often become complex and completely baffling, a result not lost on Jabir who concludes:

> One must not explain this art in obscure words only; on the other hand, one must not explain it so clearly that all may understand it. I therefore teach it in such a way that nothing will remain hidden to the wise man, even though it may strike mediocre minds as quite obscure; the foolish and the ignorant, for their part, will understand none of it at all.[4]

Abu Musa Jabir Ibn Hayyan claimed that all of his alchemical spiritual knowledge was no more than an articulation of his master Jafar's original teachings. If his legacy is in truth simply the transmission of his teacher's illumination, at the very least the endurance of Jabir's work and its continued influence upon Alchemy in the West attests to the worthiness of the student. If, on the other hand, Jabir's contribution to al-Kimia lies in his ability to cause a *projection* of the gold of the teacher's words resulting in more gold by expanding on Jafar's themes with his own vial of the Red Elixir, then he honors the process by disappearing into it.

4. Titus Burckhardt, *Alchemy* (London: Stuart & Watkins, 1967), p30.

4

ABU'L-FAIZ THAUBAN IBN EBRAHIM AL-MESRI: DHO L'NUN

Once a saintly dervish took passage in a ship in which some gold was lost. One by one the passengers were searched, and although the gold was not found, everyone decided to blame the dervish. They abused him mercilessly and yet he remained silent until he finally exclaimed, 'Oh, God, Thou knowest!' Immediately thousands and thousands of fish emerged, each with a perfect pearl in its mouth. The dervish collected a quantity of the pearls and dropped them on board the ship, and then he sprang aloft, sitting high in the air like a king. The people on the ship were amazed and exclaimed that the pearls were from God, and belonged to no one else. High above them before the ship's mast the dervish said, 'Begone! The ship for you, God for me, so that a beggerly thief may not be in your company! I am happy, being united with Him and separated from His creatures.' And that is how this dervish came to be called Dho l'Nun (The Fish).[1]

Adapted from Rumi's *Mathnawi*

THE SYMBOLISM OF AN UPTURNED MOUTH with something in it is apparent in the Arabic letter *Nuun* (which looks like a bowl-shaped U with a dot above it). The Hebrew letter *Nun* resembles a fish hook and literally means *the fish*, the highest embodiment

1. The *Mathnawi* of Jalalu'ddin Rumi, 3 vols., trans. by Reynold A. Nicholson (Cambridge: E.J.W. Gibb Memorial Trust, 1926), verses 3478–3491. The version of this same story found in 'Attar is from Hojwiri.

springing out of *Mem*, the letter signifying water. *Nun* symbolizes the combustion of fluids that form the quintessence. The Hebrew word for man is *Ish*. In the Hermetic symbol of the 'Grand Man,' the feet are two fishes, Sol and Luna, the basis for *under*standing.[2]

The human body is 95 percent water and symbolizes the Great [passive] Sea while the inner [active] Spirit is therefore symbolized as a 'Fish' in the Great Sea. *'By their fruits ye shall know them'*: The fruit of the sea [the body] is the fish (the mind, wisdom, knowledge). *'And the Spirit of God was moving over the face of the waters'* (Gen. 2).

In the section of Rumi's *Mathnawi* immediately preceding the one mentioned above, from verses 3472–3475, Rumi makes explicit reference to alchemical symbolism, as if to preface the famous anecdote about Dho l'Nun that immediately follows with a hint,

> Do service to the elixir, like copper: endure oppression, O heart, from him that holds the heart in fee.[3]

Dho l'Nun (d. 859), 'the physician of the afflicted and the sovereign prescriber of the sages,'[4] was a legendary Sufi, Thaumaturge, and Alchemist born of Nubian parents in Ikhmim in upper Egypt. Although not much is known of his life, it is known that he studied under various teachers and traveled extensively in Arabia and Syria. In the *ar-Risala fi'ilm at-Tassawuf* by Abu'l-Qasim al-Qushayri (Cairo 1912), he is called the 'unique authority of his time in scholarship and piety and mystical state and culture.' The *Fihrist* mentions two of his works among alchemical scriptures, although the bulk of the works attributed to him are for the most part apocryphal. He is reputed to have been a major link in the transmission of the spiritual sciences of ancient Egypt. He was 'accused' of being a philosopher and an alchemist, and the genuineness of his mystical state was sometimes doubted.

2. For an illustration of the 'Grand Man' see *Paracelsus: Selected Writings* (paperback ed.), Jolande Jacobi, ed., trans. by Norbert Guterman (Princeton: Princeton University Press, 1988), cover illustration.

3. *Mathnawi*: verse 3475.

4. Attar, Farid al-Din, *Tadhkirat al-Auliya*, A.J. Arberry, tr. (New York: Viking Press, 1990), from the anecdote: 'Dho l'Nun and the pious disciple', pp92–93.

The last conclusion may have been encouraged by Dho l'Nun himself. It is known that he traveled the way of the *malamatiyya*, the path of blame. The fact is made obvious in the preceding anecdote, in which, for some reason, perhaps because of his dervish robe, he is singled out of all the passengers on the ship and identified as the thieving culprit —an accusation he finally accepts!

In another anecdote, a dervish comes to Dho l'Nun to complain that after forty years of as many *chillas* (retreats), he has not received any attention from God. Dho l'Nun counsels that perhaps if the man were to anger God by skipping his evening prayers that very night, God may grant him notice. The pious dervish finds that he cannot be negligent as advised and makes his prayer. Later that night he dreams of the Prophet who tells him that God greets him and gives him benefit for his forty years of obedience, but says to notify 'that bandit and pretender' Dho l'Nun that 'If I do not expose your shame before all the city, then I am not your Lord.' When the man awoke and went to Dho l'Nun, he said to him, 'God sends you greeting and declares you a pretender and a liar.' Dho l'Nun rolled over and over with joy and wept ecstatically.[5] Ibn 'Arabi[6] considered the *malamatiyya* to be the perfect mystical elect chosen of God.[7]

Al-Kalabadhi reported that when Dho l'Nun was asked, 'What is the end of the knowers?' He answered, 'When he is as he was where he was before he was.'[8] He believed affliction to be indispensable to man's spiritual development and said: 'It is the salt of the faithful, and when the salt lacks, the faithful become rotten.'[9] Dho l'Nun was the first to posit the theory of *marifa*, intuitive knowledge of God or gnosis, as opposed to *'ilm*, discursive learning and knowledge. Many sayings about Love and Intimacy are attributed to him. There are also many anecdotes about Dho l'Nun in 'Attar's *Tadhkirat al-Auliya* with veiled or direct reference to al-Kimia. We will end this look at the life of Dho l'Nun with two versions of these anecdotes fairly

5. Ibid.
6. (d. 1240). See chap. 8.
7. See Chodkiewicz, Michel, *An Ocean Without Shore: Ibn Arabi, The Book and the Law* (Albany: SUNY Press, 1993).
8. Untraced.
9. From Abu Nu'aym al-Isfahani, *Hilyat ul-Auliya*, 10 vols., Cairo, 1932.

representative of the group:

> Once a young man approached Dho l'Nun with some gold he wanted to give to the dervishes. After the dervishes had spent the money, one day an emergency arose and the young man commented that it was a pity that he did not possess another quantity of gold to give to this company.
>
> When Dho l'Nun heard him say this, he realized that the young man was still attached to the world and had not yet fully realized the mystic way.
>
> He instructed the young man to go to a certain druggist and purchase an amount of a particular medicine. When he returned, Dho l'Nun instructed him to grind the medicine up with mortar and pestle, to add a little oil, and to then make a paste. He told him to roll this paste into pellets and then to pierce each pellet with a needle. When this was done, the young man brought the pellets to Dho l'Nun, who rubbed them in his hands awhile and then he breathed on them, after which they turned into three beautiful rubies.
>
> He instructed the young man to have them appraised, after which he returned with the rubies, assured of their worth. Dho l'Nun then told him to return the rubies to the mortar, to pound them, and then throw them into the water.
>
> When he had done this, Dho l'Nun told him that the dervishes were not hungry from lack of bread, that this was their free choice. At this the young man repented, his soul awoke, and he no longer valued anything of this world.[10]

❅

A man once came to Dho l'Nun saying that he had a debt he could not pay. Dho l'Nun picked up a rock from the ground and handed it

---

10. *Tadhkirat al-Auliya*, pp 95–96.

to him. It had turned into an emerald that the man sold and then paid his debt.[11]

Dho l'Nun was an Egyptian Sufi master who became an alchemical vehicle for the transmission of the original knowledge of ancient *Kem*. He apparently gained this knowledge directly by virtue of his birthright alone.

Unlike Arab and Persian Sufis and alchemists, Dho l'Nun was able to bypass the synthesizing influences of Hellenistic Alexandria and the subsequent legacy of hermetic lore by accessing the *art* directly from the source of the Nile. He became the unsurpassed Master of his age whose influences included ingredients of al-Kimia, Sufism, and *malamatiyya*. Dho l'Nun represented the *gold in its bath, the fish* 'which swims in our philosophic water.'[12]

11. Ibid., p97.

12. *Cosmopolite* or *Nouvelle Lumiere Chymique, Traite du Sel* (Paris: J. d'Houry, 1669), p76.

5

ABU BAKR MUHAMMAD ZAKARIYYA AR-RAZI

The shining sun
and the glittering full moon
shine and glitter
from the trunk of this tree.
Brilliant birds
are there sporting happily.
Sporting there are doves
and peacocks of all kinds.

[Manichaean] Paradise of Light (Middle Persian)

ABU BAKR MUHAMMAD ZAKARIYYA AR-RAZI (d. 925) is not to be confused with other famous Razi's such as Najm al-Din Razi, author of *Mersad al-ebad men al-mabda ela l-ma'ad*, 'The Path of God's Bondsmen from the Origin of Return.' Certain alchemical texts use other western transliterations of the former Razi's name such as 'Rhazes' and 'Rhasis'.[1]

Abu Bakr Muhammad Zakariyya ar-Razi was a Persian born in Rayy (hence the name Razi) near Tehran where he studied logic, metaphysics, poetry, and music. At age thirty he went to Baghdad to study medicine. The study of medicine at this time also included the study of Alchemy, so it may be safely concluded that the anonymous pharmacist who became Razi's master in medicine also initiated him into the art of al-Kimia.

---

1. See for example *Bacstrom's Alchemical Anthology* (Edmonds: The Alchemical Press), p9, et. al.

Razi had an extremely well equipped laboratory and followed all of the essentials of Jabir's systems. In one area in particular, he expanded upon Jabir's theory. Razi added a third principle, philosophically representing Spirit as Mind, and Mercury as Soul, while adding Salt as the principle of crystallization or Body.

Razi differentiated five external principles related to Plato's *Timaeus* in its later Alexandrian interpretation: Creator, Soul, Matter, Time, and Space. He seems to have been influenced by Platonism on the one hand and Manichaeanism on the other. Razi was and is to this day recognized as a universal thinker who pursued all the sciences including astronomy, theology, and music.

Perhaps due to his far-reaching 'scientific' interests in general, it is not surprising that Razi formulated an atomic theory.[2] He saw all substances as composed of indivisible elements of a certain size and indestructibility. The space between the elements determined the form of Nature: Fire, Water, Earth, Air. Their proximity to each other fixed the weight of the atoms and decided whether the appearance will be transparent or opaque, of what color, and if soft or hard. Spatial relations between atoms also determined the type of movement: Fire and Air, UP; Earth and Water, DOWN.

Razi's descriptions of the alchemical processes were closely studied and put into practice by later European alchemists including Nicolas Flamel and Paracelsus.

Razi was, like Jabir, a prolific author. Some of his titles include: *Liber Pestilentiae*; *al-Kitab al-Mansuri*; *Book on the Secrets of Healing*;

---

2. The term 'atom' in Greek is defined as 'not cuttable' and is derived from Democritus (c. 400 BC) who theorized that if matter were *divided* into smaller and smaller pieces, a point would be reached where division was no longer possible. The concepts of elementary particles according to modern nuclear physics are undergoing changes challenging (and defining/depending upon) the human imagination. Alchemy differs from modern chemistry in the view that the presumed stability of the 'elements' is in fact an instability subject to the laws of nature in which nothing but change is 'stable'. This point of view recognizes the transmutation of matter as a natural process accelerated by the artisan of al-Kimia.

As Nature is extremely subtle and penetrating in her manifestations she cannot be used without the Art. Indeed, she does not produce anything that is perfect in itself, but man must make it perfect, and this perfecting is called alchemy.

PARACELSUS

How to Take Medicine without Nausea; On the Disease of the Joints; The Book of Experiments; Treatise on the Stone; Book of the Secret of Secrets; Book of Sixty Animals; and the encyclopedic *al-Hawi*, among many others. In one text, he gives this prescription for insomnia:

> Boil left eye of a porcupine in oil, then place a drop of oil in patient's ear-sleep will follow.

Razi was well known as a physician who recognized the role that self-suggestion or psychosomatic medicine plays in healing. He wrote a treatise explaining why certain old wives remedies, and the advice and practice of so-called quacks, laymen, and other untrained practitioners often work when more conventional methods fail.

Albertus Magnus[3] praised his works; however his contemporary al-Firabi,[4] and later al-Biruni criticized him as a philosopher. Perhaps they followed some of his medical advice: 'To relieve sexual problems, eat a toad.'

Ar-Razi was able to expand upon some of the theories of Jabir, thus making him heir to the gnosis of Jafar as-Sadiq. He rescued folk medicine from the profane, and restored its sacred status in the pantheon of al-Kimia. By adding Salt to the Philosophic concepts of Sulphur and Mercury he realized the holy alchemic Trinity.

Salt would become the preoccupation of the generations of alchemists that followed Razi, culminating in the works of the twentieth-century adept(s?) R.A. Schwaller de Lubicz and Fulcanelli.

---

3. See Albertus Magnus, *The Book of Secrets of Albertus Magnus of the Virtues of Herbs, Stones, & Certain Beasts also A Book of the Marvels of the World*, Michael R. Best, ed., (Oxford: Oxford University Press, 1973). In these works and others, ar-Razi's influence on Albertus Magnus is apparent, especially in passages such as: 'And if any man shall have many Eels in a wine vessel, and they be suffered to die in it, if any man drink of it, he shall abhor wine for a year, and by chance evermore.' (pp96–97).

4. For a brief discussion of al-Firabi, who is identified as a Sufi and an Alchemist, as well as being regarded: 'as the great commentator and follower of Aristotle" (page 14) see: S.H. Nasr, *Three Muslim Sages* (Delmar: Caravan, 1976), pp14–18. Al-Biruni is also mentioned in this discussion in footnote 29.

6

HAKIM ABU'ALI AL-HUSAYN ABD ALLAH IBN SINA

Hakim Abu'Ali al-Husayn Abd Allah Ibn Sina, known as simply Ibn Sina, or Avicenna, was born of a Turkish mother and a Persian father in a village near Bukhara in what was later called the Uzbek S.S.R. or Afghanistan. In c. 980, Bukhara was the politically and culturally Islamic capital of the Samanid dynasty, and the majority of it's population were Persian.

By age ten Ibn Sina was a *hafiz*, one who knows the entire Qur'an by heart, and was an exceptional student of poetry, geometry, arithmetic, law, logic, and especially medicine. He studied the *Isagoge* of Porphyry, and the propositions of Euclid. By the age of seventeen, he was the personal physician of a local regional ruler. He was very close to his father, an Ismaili.[1] After his father's death, Ibn Sina, at age twenty-one, became a wanderer. In his lifetime he traveled widely and lived in many places in Persia including Merv and Kazwin. He settled in Isfahan, where he was a vizier, and later he became vizier in Hamadan, where he died in the year 1037. In Hamadan, mutinying soldiers demanded that he be put to death, and he was forced to make a hasty escape in disguise. It has been said that he led a rather hedonistic lifestyle spending his last days in pious exercises and repentance.

1. See chapter 7 of the present work, 'Ismailis, Sufis, Malamatiyya, and al-Kimia' for more information on the Ismailis.

Ibn Sina wrote 276 books on natural history, physics, alchemistry, music, mathematics, economics, moral and ethical questions, and medicine, including the *ash-Shifa*, or *Healing*, also known in Europe—where Ibn Sina was called the 'Prince of Physicians'—as the *Sanatio*.

His most famous and influential work, however, was the encyclopedic *al-Qanun fi al-Tibb* or the *Canon of Medicine*,[2] which contains one million words. The Encyclopedia Britannica called the *Canon* 'the single most famous book in the history of medicine, East or West.' The *Canon* has been long considered the authority for all therapeutics. Its importance and influence is extraordinary, resulting in the founding of botany, the organization of pharmacy, and countless other contributions to the field of general medicine.

Ibn Sina felt, like Galen before him, that the five senses of taste, touch, hearing, sight, and smell have five counterpart inner senses localized in the brain; the senses of combination and image-forming in the forebrain; the emotional responses in the mid-brain; and the fifth inner sense, memory, in the back brain. For Ibn Sina, the evaluation of 'dis-ease' was incomplete until and unless all components of a person's life had been included in the 'dia-gnosis.' His evaluation anticipates modern holistic medicine by nearly 1,000 years. In fact, medical practice based on Ibn Sina's *Canon* has been in continuous use and known the world over as *Unani Tibb* or simply as the *Tibb* system.[3]

Ibn Sina also wrote a major work concerning Alchemy entitled *Liber abuali abincine de anima, in arte alchimiae.* In this work he lists real and mythical alchemists, beginning with Adam, Noah, Idris, and Moses. Among the latter-day alchemists he mentions is his own alchemical master, Jacob the Jew:

2. See O. Cameron Gruner, M.D., *A Treatise on the Canon of Medicine of Avicenna Incorporating a Translation of the First Book* (New York: Augustus M. Kelly, 1970).
3. See Hakim G. M. Chishti, *The Traditional Healer's Handbook: A Classic Guide to the Medicine of Avicenna* (Rochester: Healing Arts Press, 1988), and Shaykh Hakim Moinuddin Chishti, *The Book of Sufi Healing* (Rochester: Inner Traditions, 1991).

Jacob the Jew, a man of penetrating mind, also taught me many things, and I shall repeat to you what he taught me: if you want to be a philosopher of nature, to whichever religion you belong, listen to the instructed man of whatever religion, because the law of the philosophers says: thou shalt not kill, thou shalt not steal, thou shalt not commit adultery, do unto others as you do to yourself, and don't utter blasphemies.[4]

As an alchemist, Ibn Sina was familiar with Razi, but he apparently did not ascribe to Jabir's contention that base metals could be transmuted into gold. He did, however, believe in the *elixir* as a cure-all, as the panacea capable of universal medicinal efficacy.

Ibn Sina was most certainly a mystic.[5] He has, however, been historically considered by most Sufi mystics as a representative of cold reason, (*'aql*), as illustrated in this story concerning Majduddin Baghdadi (d. 1390).

He saw the Prophet in his dream and was informed by him that Ibn Sina wanted to reach God without my [Muhammad's] mediation, and I veiled him with my hand and he fell into the fire.[6]

Recalling the anecdote concerning the dervish's dream, in which Dho l'Nun was utterly condemned by Allah, perhaps Ibn Sina, like Dho l'Nun before him, followed the *malamatiyya*, the way of blame.

Lo, the friends of God, there is no fear upon them, neither do they grieve.

QUR'AN (10:63)

The *Filum Ariadnae* states,

Without fire, the Matter is useless and the Philosophical Mercury is a chimera that lives only in the imagination. It is on the rule of Fire that everything depends.[7]

---

4. See Marcellin P. E. Berthelot, *La chemie au moyen age*, Paris, 1893, 1:302–2.

5. See Henri Corbin's *Avicenna and the Visionary Recital*, New York and London, 1960, and *Three Muslim Sages*. op. cit.

6. Maulana 'Abdurrahman Jami, *Nafat al-uns*, ed. M. Tauhidipur, Tehran, 1957, p 427.

7. *Filum Ariadne.*

De Givry adds:

> The fire of the Sages is the only instrument that can work this sublimation: no philosopher has ever overtly revealed this secret Fire, who does not understand must stop here and ask God to illuminate him.[8]

The fire used in the alchemical process known as *calcination*, a term previously encountered in relation to Jafar As-Sadiq, must be of the kind that will *consume completely* in order to produce the purified *salt*, which when recombined with the sulphur and mercury will make the *elixir* and/or the 'stone of the wise', a spiritualized matter indeed!

Sufi mystics have often used the apparent opposition between Love ('*eshq*), on one hand, and Reason ('*aql*), on the other, to illustrate that annihilation or *fana* in God cannot be obtained through intellectual means. They point out how *fana* requires an experiential approach that utterly departs from 'book-learning.' This proceeds from the origin of the Qu'ran, revealed to the 'unlettered' (*ummi*) Prophet Muhammad through dramatic experience filled with wonder and grace.

Reason is vindicated once it surrenders to the *fire* of Love and becomes Love's ingredient or ally, if not its slave. The general doctrine of Unity implies that everything in creation has a place and function. This doctrine in itself negates any invented opposition found between concepts. Annihilation, *fana*, denies anything conceptual, thus it can be surmised that teaching vehicles or stories are simply springboards into the infinite, boundless, non-conceptual Mystery. The point of setting up such an opposition is to arrive *with God's feet*, and not one's own, 'Then I am his hearing through which he hears, his sight through which he sees, and his hand by which he grasps' (*Hadith Qudsi*), and as in al-Qur'an (8:17): 'You did not throw when you threw, but God threw.'

The importance of the medical legacy of Ibn Sina cannot be overestimated. His life was filled with controversy, yet even the legend of it has merit for students of Sufism who overlook the subtle points

8. Grillo de Givry, *Muses des sorciers, mages et alchimistes*, Paris, 1929, p 413.

that upon closer examination yield greater value. Hermetic lore generally admits to a dichotomy between ordinary knowledge and
secret knowledge. Plato, who was influenced greatly by the preceding school of Pythagorean thought, made a distinction separating
the common interpretation and that of the elect few by distinguish-
ing between *doxa* and *episteme*. This distinction, a form of Qabala
related to systems like *jafr*, has been handed down by all initiatory
chains East and West. Seen by some as a form of elitism as in who,
on the one hand, belong to the vast majority of humanity only seeing the outer appearance of words as symbols, for example; and
those among the elect few who not only see beyond the obvious use
of language, but who also reject the etymology of the word and seek
a basic and profound symbol found in the forms of Nature. It is in
this book of Nature that Ibn Sina found the inspiration for his
Canon, and for the Alchemy of his life's work.

7

ISMAILIS, SUFIS, MALAMATIYYA, AND AL-KIMIA

Ta'wil: To reveal the occult, to occultate the apparent.

HENRY CORBIN

SO FAR AN ATTEMPT HAS BEEN MADE to point to possible connections and correspondences between the historical concepts and ideas of esoteric Islam and al-Kimia by describing the lives and works of some of the most outstanding Islamic alchemists. No doubt these prolific authors and profound mystics share other similarities as well. Let us now look at a few more of the many connections these personages share. Hopefully it is clear that what they may seem to hold in common on the contrary proves the unique and sublime reality of each individual.

The sixth Shi'ite Imam Jafar as-Sadiq[1] had two sons, Ismail and Musa. Ismail died before his father, and Jafar then proclaimed Musa to become his successor.

Before his death, however, Ismail declared his son, Jafar's grandson, Muhammad ibn Ismail, to become the next Imam. The followers of Ismail, in accordance with this declaration, after Ismail's death, recognized in turn his son -also named Ismail, not his uncle Musa, as the seventh Shi'ite Imam. This group is known as the Seven Imam Shi'ites (Seveners, or *saba'iyyah*), better known as the Ismailis, who, despite their break with Jafar over his choice of successor nevertheless include him in their *silsilah* or chain of initiation.

---

1. See the present work, chapter two, 'Jafar as-Sadiq'.

The successors of Musa continued to lead the orthodox Shi'ite branch of Islam up to the twelfth Imam, who disappeared without trace and is still believed to live in occultation on the spiritual plane. He is the Hidden Imam, the *Madhi* 'who is guided' and who, it is said, will appear at the end of time to fill the world with justice. Access to this Hidden Imam is an internal affair of the heart potentially available to all believers who ascribe to his incorporeal existence. In some Sufi orders, the identification of the *murid* with the *murshid* or the disciple with the Master is analogous to this relationship in 'Twelver' Shi'ism.

The Ismaili branch flourished as a secret initiatory line including extremist Shi'ite revolutionaries and mystics. Perhaps the most colorful and legendary figure is the infamous Hasan i-Sabbah (d. 1124), the Old Man of the Mountain, whose army of alleged hashish-smoking assassins terrorized the eleventh-century landscape from their mountaintop fortress at Alamut (Eagle's Nest). Hasan I-Sabbah's great-grandson, also named Hasan, proclaimed the *Qiyamat*, or great Resurrection, at Alamut on the seventeenth day of Ramazan, the annual month-long Islamic fast.

For Ismailis, the *Qiyamat* symbolizes the end of time and also the end of all religious law. Hasan on this day effectively broke the chains of Islamic law by ordering all to break their fast with food and wine, the latter a substance expressly forbidden by the Qur'an for consumption at any time.

It is not hard to connect the significance of this action taken by Hasan with the fulfillment of the duty of the Hidden Imam *who will appear at the end of time*. Ismailis perhaps felt that the *Qiyamat* amounted to the manifestation of prophecy, and yet for the mainstream Shi'ite the whole affair amounted to a vile and contemptible heresy.

Referring to the end of Time: 'The Hour will not take place until two parties fight each other with one and the same aim.'[2] (The Prophet Muhammad)

2. Thomas Cleary, *The Wisdom of the Prophet* (Boston: Shambala Publications, 1994), p93.

Jabir Ibn Hayyan (b. between 721–730),[3] the disciple of Jafar as-Sadiq in Shi'ism, Sufism, and al-Kimia, foresaw Hasan's declaration of the *Qiyamat* when he described the Glorious One. The Glorious One was said to be an ex-patriot come from afar who would require no long initiation or Master. He proclaims the esoteric meaning of the end of religion and the end of linear time with the announcement of Eternal Life, spoken in an *immaterial diction.*[4]

Sufi poets often use terms like 'wine,' previously mentioned in connection with the *Qiyamat*, to describe a spiritual substance with unique qualities, and alchemists use elliptical and often poetic terms to describe their processes. Both make use of multi-layered symbolic language to conceal a unifying and underlying teaching or truth designed to initiate the receptive and confound the literal-minded. This initiatory vocabulary, with possible roots in Jafar as-Sadiq's *jafr*,[5] provides a non-linear point of departure into the mystic unknowing for the attentive recipient, in some ways much like the function of the *Qiyamat* in Ismailism.

The Ismaili interpretation of the general Shia use of *taqiyyah* or dissimulation involved protecting the sacred lore from profane ears and became an internal discipline supporting the hierarchy. The secret sacred lore was thus protected at every level from those not yet ready for further initiation into the Mysteries. Hermeticism of this sort exists in some Sufi forms of instruction in which the Master, aided or identified with the grace or *barakat* of God, guides the disciple through various stages and stations, a process which also often simultaneously unlocks the symbolism inherent and buried in Sufi texts. An analogous situation is found in the initiatory aspects of al-Kimia. In each separate case, the initiate is aided by God and God's representative the Master, and is supported by texts which open first intellectually, and then experientially.

3. See the present work, chapter three, 'Jabir Ibn Hayyan'.

4. For more on Jabir's prophecy concerning the Glorious One, see Henry Corbin, *Cyclical Time and Ismaili Gnosis* (London: Kegan Paul, 1983), p126.

5. See the present work, chapter two, 'Jafar as-Sadiq'; and chapter three, 'Jabir Ibn Hayyan', for more on *jafr* and its legacy.

In Jabir's work The Glorious One,[6] a version of *jafr* is used to describe the basis of what would become Twelver Shi'ism, the predominate Shi'ism in Iran today. By using Jabir as a reference point, Twelver Shi'ism considers itself to be a return to 'primitive Shi'ism'. Reflecting the same use of single letters as in the Qur'an, The Glorious One begins with the letters *'Ayn*, symbolizing in this system 'Ali; *Sin*, symbolizing Salman the Persian, adopted into the Prophet's household; and *Mim*, symbolizing Muhammad.

The order of the use of these particular letters and the human mystical counterparts they symbolize clearly points to the preference and precedence of the Imam in Twelver Shi'ism.

The Ismailis to this day are considered to be heretics by orthodox Shi'ism, in itself regarded as heresy by most Sunni Muslims. This places them, by association only perhaps, in the path of the *malamatiyya*, the 'blameworthy' ones previously mentioned in relation to the lives of Dho l'Nun and Ibn Sina.

Ibn Sina's father and brother were both Ismailis. Although Ibn Sina was not considered an Ismaili himself, this close association points to a possible sympathy on his part. The apparent trauma at his father's death led him from court physician to wanderer at an early age. Perhaps this familial connection supplied enough evidence to support the condemnation he suffered from more mainstream Sufis like al-Ghazzali and al-Farabi, who were both mystics working with their own correspondences to the subject at hand.

Other Sufi adepts are mentioned in the Ismaili *silsilah* alongside Jafar as-Sadiq, such as Shams al-Din Tabrizi, and Jalalludin Rumi, the famous author of the *Mathnawi*, also known as the 'Persian Qu'ran'.[7]

Rumi, a disciple of Shams al-Din Tabrizi, and Ibn 'Arabi, whose stepson Sadruddin Qunawi was a great friend of Rumi's, profoundly influenced the life and work of the mystic Fakhruddin 'Iraqi.[8]

6. Ibid.

7. Reynold A. Nicholson, *The Mathnawi of Jalalu'ddin Rumi*, 3 vols. (Cambridge: E.J.W. Gibb Memorial Trust, 1926).

8. See William C. Chittick and Peter Lamborn Wilson, *Fakhruddin 'Iraqi-Divine Flashes* (New York, NY: Paulist Press, 1982). This is an English rendering of 'Iraqi's *Lama'at*, an esoteric, expressive, and poetic commentary on the doctrine of Ibn

'Iraqi's initial connection with Sufism came from his association with a group of wandering *qalandars*, another group of outsiders who by tending to disregard all outward socially accepted norms, consistently incurred the wrath and indignation of the orthodox Islamic community. In reality, the *qalandars'* and the *malamatiyyas'* position must be viewed as the apogee of the blameworthy, and they may indeed be considered some of the 'hidden' sublime caretakers of the faith.

When reviewing the Shi'ites, the Ismailis, the Sufis, and even the majority of mainstream Muslims, the Sunnis, and the many other branches and manifestations of Islam, it is noteworthy to remember the words of the Prophet Muhammad uttered upon returning from the lesser *jihad* (holy struggle of physical conflict with those opposing Islam) to the greater *jihad* (each individual's response to living within the religion of God):

> O People, turn to God in repentance, and seek forgiveness of God. Indeed, I repent a hundred times a day.

Some Sufis believe that the act of asking anything of God results in being conscious of self, and unconscious of God. Duality of any sort is anathema in strictly monotheistic Islam and denies that whatever comes, good or bad, is ultimately God's will. To realize this subtle point, one must then repent of repentance and surrender to a (non) conceptualization of the ultimate Unity of Being, the *wahdat al-wujud* of Ibn 'Arabi.

> Remembering repentance at the time of remembering God is forgetting the remembrance of God.
>
> JAFAR AS-SADIQ

Dr. Javad Nurbakhsh, present Master, of the Nimatullahi Order of Sufis, writes:

'Arabi. This expression of the Sufi mystic's 'religion' of Love can be traced to Jafar as-Sadiq, and, among others, most notably Ahmad Ghazzali, brother of Abu Hamid al-Ghazzali, and Master of the martyred mystic 'A'in al-Qudat al-Hamadhani. See also Ahmad Ghazzali, *Sawanih: Inspirations from the World of Pure Spirits*, trans. Nasrollah Pourjavady (London: KPI Limited, 1986).

Thus may I shatter this talisman 'La,'[9]
And refrain forever from further repentance.'

In the eighteenth and nineteenth centuries, a number of shaykhs and darvishes of the Nimatullahi Sufi Order in Persia were executed for heresy. Several of the order's members at this time were also high ranking Ismailis, including the Ismaili Imam, the Aga Khan. Mast Ali Shah, a Master of the Nimatullahi Order, reportedly once said of this relationship, 'I have a *murid* like the Aga Khan who himself has thousands of *murids* in most countries of the world.'[10]

One of the martyred Nimatullahi's of this period was the brilliant musician, Mushtaq Ali Shah. The Ismailis and many others were attracted to Mushtaq, drawn to the immense mystical power of his singing and *setar* playing. The attraction of the mystical harmony of music transcends the visual form and is *the* universal Pythagorean gnosis. Mushtaq had utter disregard for outer convention due to his mystical station as a *majdhoub*, one who is divinely intoxicated, or 'mad-in-the-Divine.' He was stoned to death along with a dervish disciple name Jafar(!) for allegedly singing and playing the call to prayer at the Jum'ah Masjid on the 27th Ramazan, 1792; an action warranting capital punishment in the eyes of the contemporary orthodox Muslims. Deadly force on the part of the exoteric self-appointed guardians of the faith actualizes and perpetuates the need for esoteric Hermeticism.

Of Shah Nur al-Din Ni'matullah Wali (b. 1331 in Aleppo), the Sunni founder of the Nimatullahi Order of Sufis, it was said, 'he knew the secret of al-Kimia.' Not only did his followers believe in the art of al-Kimia, they most certainly continue to believe that their founder was adept in the sacred *art*, and that he was as well a sublime and unique Sufi master.

In the nineteenth century, Ostad Gholam-Reza Shishegar, a disciple of Zuhur 'Ali Shah, a shaykh of Rida 'Ali Deccani's in Persia, is identified as a practicing alchemist. Shaykh Shishegar mysteriously

---

9. 'La' is the word 'no' in the Muslim profession of faith: 'There is no God, but God,' in which one symbolically negates the existence of all forms of divinity other than the Absolute with the word 'la'.

10. Meherally, Akbarally, *A History of the Agakhani Ismailis* (Burnaby: A.M. Trust, 1991), pp 62–63.

graces the cover of *SUFI: The Magazine of Khaniqahi Nimatullahi* (Issue 3, Autumn 1989) which gives as the date of his death 1884, with no other explanation for the use of his picture on the cover of this particular issue of the magazine.

In Sufism, and Shi'ism, as well as in one of the latter's extreme manifestations: Ismailism, and also in al-Kimia, distinctions between inner and outer, interior and exterior, *batin* and *zahir*, after a certain point lose their dualism for the aspirant in the realm of absolute Unity. For the alchemist, the exterior symbols of the book of Nature correspond exactly to what is seen 'inside,' while the fruits of alchemical work are manifested by the transmutation of the *prima materia* in every conceptual sense.

> And if all the trees in the earth were pens, and the sea, with seven more seas to help it, were ink, the words of Allah could not be exhausted.
>
> QUR'AN (31:27)

The revelations of the prophets are the congealed spiritual substances forming the living words of sacred texts. The text, then, like the teacher, is the transmuting agent, the *barzakh*, or barrier, an intermediary, which spiritualizes the aspirant *body and soul*.

The adept cannot but wait in a state of pure silence or in what the Sufis call a state of annihilation (*fana*) in God. For the alchemist this amounts to the famous prayer before the *at-tannur*, or athanor (furnace). As the old saying goes: Silence is *golden*.

This is not to say that ordinary utterance *strictly speaking* is not derived from God; however, in order for this process to adhere to the recognition of a transmutation or a *spiritualization of the matter*, there must be a recognizable difference between revelation and other forms of expression.

> 'Learn my meaning,' said he [Poimandres], 'by looking at what you yourself have in you; for in you too, the word is son, and the mind is father of the word. They are not separate from one another; for life is the union of word and mind.'[11]
>
> HERMES TRISMEGISTOS

---

11. Walter Scott, *Hermetica* (Boston: Shambala Publs, 1985), Libellus I:6, p117.

In Sufism, the Alchemy of the association of the aspirant with a dervish, initiation into an Order, and ultimately the attention of the Sufi Master changes the lead of his imperfect nature into the gold of the perfect being who has found a unique union in God.

One of the primary transmuting tools used by the Master is the inculcation of the *zikr*, a Name of God that is invoked at every opportunity. Ibn 'Arabi states that the person mindful of the *zikr* should regard it as an act of profound and personal worship. The invoker should not dwell on the meaning or even the understanding of the remembrance, but should rather commit the *zikr* to practice automatically in order for it to cause a spiritual effect.

> If the truths [realities] were manifest, the religious laws would be naught. As [for example], when copper becomes gold or was gold originally, it does not need the alchemy which is the Law, nor need it rub itself upon the philosopher's stone, which [operation] is the Path; [for] as has been said, it is unseemly to demand a guide after arrival at the goal, and blameworthy to discard the guide before arrival at the goal. In short, the Law is like learning the theory of alchemy from a teacher or a book, and the Path is [like] making use of chemicals and rubbing the copper upon the philosopher's stone, and the Truth is [like] the transmutation of the copper into the gold. Those who know alchemy rejoice in their knowledge of it, saying, 'We know the theory of this science'; and those who practice it rejoice in their practice of it, saying, 'We perform such works'; and those who have experienced the reality rejoice in the reality, saying, 'We have become gold and are delivered from the theory and practice of alchemy: we are God's freedmen.'[12]

> JALLALUDIN RUMI

Our contemporary world-view consistently seeks to separate and categorize in order to form opinions engendering debate and false notions of individuality and originality. Systems such as *jafr* evolve

12. Reynold A. Nicholson, ed. and trans., *The Mathnawi* (Cambridge: E.J.W. Gibb Memorial, 1990), Introduction to bk. v, p3.

from the unified exegesis of ancient philosophical as well as practical Hermeticism springing directly from the human being's intuition of the wholeness of multiplicity. Al-Kimia provides a way to synthesize all sciences and to integrate the intellectual and spiritual faculties of the human being. Potentially, religion may become the meaningful vehicle that ultimately articulates the individual's search for origin through perpetual freshness of revelation. The tension between arbitrary distinctions such as 'outer' and 'inner' work can only be resolved in a mystical apprehension of Oneness. Esoteric Islam possesses a 1,400-year-old 'latter-day' revelation with the potential to alchemically produce this effect.

II

THE ARC OF DESCENT

8

SHU'AYB IBN AL-HUSAYN
AL'ANSARI ABU MADYAN

That beaming light which turned the black heart to gold is an alchemy
which lies in association with darvishes.

HAFEZ

Glory be to Him who has not made any sign leading to His saints save
as a sign leading to Himself, and who has joined no one to them
except him whom God wants to join to Himself.

IBN 'ATA 'ALLAH, from the Kitab al-Hikam

Mercy descends at the mention of the pious.

MUHAMMAD

We have forgiven you of your sins, that which precedes and that which
follows.

QUR'AN (48:2)

'That which precedes' may apply to all human beings who have lived
in the period of occultation of the 'Muhammadan Reality' of which
previous prophets had been only substitutes in this world; 'that which
follows' may apply to all those who live from the moment that this
Muhammadan Reality became manifest in the person of Muhammad.[1]

MICHEL CHODKIEWICZ

---

1. Michel Chodkiewicz, *An Ocean Without Shore: Ibn Arabi, the Book, and the
Law* (Albany: SUNY Press, 1993), p44.

Those who live by the example of the last prophet and follow God's commandments as revealed in al-Qu'ran will become the *walis*, the Friends of God, the Saints of the ages and 'that which follows.'

Ibn Arabi, the self-revealed Seal of Muhammadan Sainthood, the Shaykh al-Akbar, The Greatest of Teachers, mentions one saint more often than any of his other teachers in his vast corpus of mystical writings. This Shaykh of the greatest of Shaykhs was named Shu'ayb ibn al-Husayn al-'Ansari Abu Madyan (1126-1198), also known as Abu Madyan Shu'ayb or Abu Madyan Sho'aib Maghrebi, and also Abu Madyan al-Andalusi. In the *isnad of the tariq* of the Darqawi Order of Sufis the title *Ghawth*, a *qutb* who heals, a granter of requests characterized by vast generosity, is added to his name. Abu Madyan Sho'aib *Maghrebi* or 'of the west,' is the patron Sufi saint of *all* the West, and consequently is of major importance to the growing darvish community in North America. He is referred to most often as, simply, Abu Madyan.

Abu Madyan is found in the Nimatullahi *silsilah* or chain of the initiatory succession of Sufi masters whose esoteric teaching is transmitted through each succeeding master beginning with Muhammad, originally receiving initiation from Jabriel, the angel and messenger of Allah.

Abu Madyan was born in 1126 near Seville, Spain, into a poor family. He was a shepherd as a youth, and later in Morocco he apprenticed himself to a weaver. He spent most of his life unable to read or write, thus qualifying himself as *ummi*. He continually sought out spiritual guides such as Abu-l-Hasan ibn Harzihim, one of his first teachers found while traveling through Fez. In Fez, Abu Madyan worked to support himself by weaving but lived in such a perpetual state of poverty that his fellow darvishes once took pity on him and hid a sum of money in his clothing. Each night he would go to the side of the Zalagh mountain outside Fez to meditate at a place later known as the *khalwah*, or retreat, of Abu Madyan. It is said that a gazelle at this spot would visit him as he meditated. The night he arrived for meditation with the money hidden in his clothing, the gazelle avoided him, and the village dogs began to bark. Sensing something amiss, he discovered the money and reportedly said, 'It was because of this uncleanness that the gazelle fled.' The gazelle is symbolic of the attraction of the beautiful Beloved, as Hafez writes:

'O Zephyr, kindly tell that graceful gazelle
That it was she who set me wandering
in the mountains and the desert.'[2]

This story is an illustration of how Abu Madyan, even at this early stage of his spiritual journeying as a *salik* or wayfarer on the path had grown close enough to God to be independent of, if not undisturbed by, worldly concerns.

Abu Madyan soon after became the disciple of Abu Ya'za Yalannur ibn Maymum al-Gharbi, a Dukkala Berber, who lived at Fez and also at Taghyah.

Abu Ya'za, was 'on the heart of Moses.' When Moses returned from his Lord, God clothed his face in a blindingly fierce light. Once, when Abu Madyan looked upon this shaykh, he went blind from the light of Moses he saw there, until

Abu Madyan rubbed his eyes with the garment that Abu Ya'za was wearing and recovered his sight.[3]

Abu Madyan, according to some accounts,[4] apparently met another of his teachers, 'Abdo'l-Qader Gilani, in Mecca. Gilani was the famous mystic and founder of the Qaderi Order of darvishes. According to Martin Lings,[5] Abu Madyan was in Baghdad during the lifetime of 'Abdo'l-Qader and was invested with the *khirqa* or initiatic mantle by him. Shaykh 'Abdullah Yafi'i was the master of Sayyid Nur al-Din Shah Ni'matullah Wali, the previously mentioned founder of the Nimatullahi Sufi Order.[6] He was also the spiritual

2. Javad Nurbakhsh, *Sufi Symbolism*, 12 vols. (New York: Khaniqahi-Nimatullahi, 1986–1995), vol. 4, p153.

3. Michel Chodkiewicz, *Seal of the Saints: Prophethood and Sainthood in the Doctrine of Ibn 'Arabi* (Cambridge: Islamic Texts Society, 1993), p74.

4. Cyril Glasse, *The Concise Encyclopedia of Islam* (San Francisco: Harper Collins, 1989), p20.

5. Martin Lings, *What is Sufism?* (Berkeley: University of California, 1975), pp112–113.

6. See present work, chap. 8, 'Ismailis, Sufis, *Malamatiyya*, and al-Kimia'.

descendent of abu Madyan through Yafi'i's master Shaykh Salih Bar-bari and his master Najm al-Din Kamal Kufi. Kufi's master Abu'l-Futuh al-Sai'di, the disciple and successor of abu Madyan, claims that 'Abdo'l- Qader Gilani and Abu Madyan were the masters of the age, of East and West respectively. In Jami's *Nafahat al-ons*,[7] he quotes Yafi'i as saying, 'Most of the masters of Yemen are linked to Shaykh 'Abdo'l-Qader and some are linked to Shaykh Abu Madyan. The latter is Master of the West and the former, that is, Shaykh 'Abdo'l-Qader, is Master of the East.' In this same work Jami relates:

One day Shaykh Abu Madyan laid his neck down in several loca-tions (indicating his own spiritual power in demonstrating something to his disciples) in the Maghreb (North Africa), declaring, 'O Lord, I bear witness before You and before Your angels that I hear and obey.' When his disciples asked why he made this declaration, he explained, 'Today in Baghdad Shaykh 'Abdo'l-Qader stated, "My foot is on the neck of every wali of God." Afterwards certain of Shaykh 'Abdo'l-Qader's disciples came from Baghdad and confirmed that 'Abdo'l-Qader had said just that at the given moment.'[8]

Louis Massignon, in his famous *Passion of al-Hallaj*,[9] states that Abu Madyan also received the *khirqa*, which often took the form of a 'patchwork cloak', from AB Turushi.

Yet another teacher of Abu Madyan, mentioned before his name in the *silsilah* of the Nimatullahi Order, was Shaykh Abu'l-Saud al-Andalusi. It is stated in *Masters of the Path*[10] that Abu Madyan was the disciple and successor of this Shaykh who is described as a *ashiq-i haqq* or lover of God, who never refused whatever came from God and never asked anything of anyone.

7. See present work, chap. 6, 'Hakim Abu-Ali al-Husayn Abd Allah Ibn Sina', note 5.
8. *Nafahat al-ons*, p528. See also Terry Graham, ''Abdo'l-Qader Gilani and the Qaderyiya Order', *SUFI Magazine*, Issue #3, pp22–28.
9. Louis Massignon, *The Passion of al-Hallaj*, 4 vols., trans. by Herbert Mason (Princeton: Princeton University Press, 1982), vol. 2, p311.
10. Javad Nurbakhsh, *Masters of the Path: A History of the Masters of the Nimat-ullahi Sufi Order* (New York: Khaniqahi-Nimatullhi, 1980), pp34–35.

A quality that Abu Madyan seems to have received from 'Abdol'l-Qader is the ability to initiate and influence his disciples through the intermediate realm, in the *barzakh*, without need of a corporeal form. Receiving the *khirqa* from 'Abdo'l-Qader (d. 1166) does not necessarily require the mediating presence of a living Qaderi master; one's personal association in the *imaginal* realm with 'Abdo'l-Qader himself is felt to be sufficient. The reverence and respect paid by innumerable pilgrims at the tombs of both Abu Madyan and 'Abdo'l-Qader Gilani to this day testify to their transmutating spiritual power.

Abu Madyan finally settled in Bougia in Algeria where he attracted a following and where he died and was buried near the outskirts of Tlemcen, in the village of al-'Ubbad, also called 'Sidi Boumedienne', in 1198 CE. His tomb remains an important and potent place of pilgrimage, as evidenced by the following accounts.

Ibn Arabi himself never met Abu Madyan in the flesh. He certainly associated with several of Abu Madyan's darvishes, learning from them, and acquiring *himma*, the burning desire of spiritual yearning, to meet the Pole of the age, which he accomplished in the following manner:

One day, during the lifetime of Abu Madyan, after I had performed the sunset prayer in my house at Seville I had a great desire to see the Shaykh Abu Madyan who was at Bugia, some forty-five days journey away. After the sunset prayer I performed two cycles of the supererogatory prayer and, as I was saying the ritual greeting (*taslim*), Abu 'Imran (al-Sadrani) came in and greeted me. I sat him down next to me and enquired where he had come from, to which he replied that he had come from Abu Madyan at Bugia. Upon my asking him when he had been with him, he replied that he had only just finished praying the sunset prayer with him. He told me that Abu Madyan had said to him, 'Certain things have occurred to the mind of Muhammad b. al-Arabi at Seville, so go at once and answer him on my behalf.' Then Abu 'Imran mentioned the wish I had had to meet Abu Madyan and told me that Abu Madyan had said, 'Tell Ibn al-Arabi that as for our meeting together in the spirit, well and good, but as for our meeting in the flesh in this world, God will not permit it. Let him however rest assured, for the time appointed for him and me lies in the security of God's mercy.[11]

Shaykh Abu'l-Abbas al-Mursi, master of Ibn 'Ata'illah, author of the famous *Kitab al-Hikam* or 'Book of Wisdom,' and direct disciple of Abu al-Hasan as-Shadhili, founder of the Shadhili order after the death of his master, 'Abd al-Salam Ibn Mashish, the direct disciple and receiver of the *khirqa* of Abu Madyan, related the following (abbreviated) vision:

Regarding the firasa [penetrating insight] of the utterly sincere, it is like my experience with my teacher (al-Shadhili) from whom I received what he had received. On that occasion, I was before the Throne [of God] and I saw Shaykh Abu Madyan to whom I said, 'Who are you, and what sciences do you possess, and what has God imparted to you?

'I' he replied, 'am head of the seven and one of the four, and seventy-one sciences are mine.'[12]

Ibn Maryam recorded that Al-Mursi related that Abu Madyan possessed seventy-one sciences, was one of the four *awtad* (lieutenants), and head of the seven *abdal* (substitutes).[13]

Sayyidi 'Abd al-Wahhab ash-Shar'ani relates in his *Tabaqat al-Kubra*, 'The Greatest Classes,' that Shaykh Abu'l Hajjaj al-Aqsuri said

I met al-Khidr, peace be upon him, in 580, so I asked him about our Shaykh Abu Madyan. He said, He is the Imam of the Siqqidun in this moment and his secret is from the will. That was given to him by Allah as a key from the secret protected by the veil of absolute purity. There is no one at this hour who gathers the secrets of the Messengers more than him.[14]

11. R.W.J. Austin, *Sufis of Andalusia* (London: George Allan & Unwin Ltd, 1970), p121.

12. Ibn al-Sabbagh, *The Mystical Teachings of al-Shadhili*, trans. by Elmer D. Douglas (Albany: SUNY at Albany, 1993), pp214–215.

13. Ahmad Baba, *Nayl al-Ibtihaj bi-tatriz al-dibaj*, Cairo, 1908.

14. Sayyidi 'Abd al-Wahhab ash-Shar'ani, *Taba qat al-Aqsuri*.

Ibn 'Ata'illah, the Shadhili master mentioned above as the author of the *Hikam* also authored a *Shahr*, a form of commentary, on a famous *Qasida*, or ode, by Abu Madyan. Ibn 'Arabi contributed a *Takhmis*, an addition or elucidation, on the same *Qasida*. What follows is the fourth line of Abu Madyan's *Qasida*, followed by Ibn 'Arabi's *Takhmis* of the same line, and then Ibn 'Ata'illah's *Shahr*.

Cling to silence unless you are questioned.

Then say, 'I have no knowledge,' and be concealed by ignorance.'

Be agreeable with them, you will be elevated by them and arrive. If they affirm you, then stand. If they obliterate you, then vanish. If they make you hungry, then be hungry. If they feed you, then eat. *Cling to silence unless you are questioned. Then say,* 'I have no knowledge,' and be concealed by ignorance.'

Cling to knowledge unless you are questioned, Then say, 'I have no knowledge,' and be concealed by ignorance. With the people of the Path, the one who clings to silence has his structure elevated and his cultivation completed. There are two types of silence: silence with the tongue, and silence with the heart. Both of them are necessary in the Path. Whoever has a silence while his tongue speaks, speaks with wisdom. Whoever has both a silent tongue and a silent heart, his secret is revealed to him in *tajalli* and his Lord speaks to him. This is the goal of silence. The Shaykh said the like of that. O wayfarer! Then cling to silence unless you are questioned. If you are questioned, then fall back on your root and your connection and say, '*I have no knowledge*', and be concealed by ignorance. Then the lights of knowledge given by Allah will shine on you. Whenever you admit your ignorance and fall back on your root, the recognition of your self will appear to you. If you recognize it, you will recognize your Lord as it is related in the *hadith*, 'Whoever recognizes his self, recognizes his Lord.' All of that is from the benefits of silence and adhering to its *adab* [precepts of courtesy]. Be silent then, and show *adab*, and cling to the door-you will be among His lovers. How excellent is that which was said:

I will not leave the door until you mend my crookedness and you accept me in spite of my defect and shortcoming. If you are pleased, then, O my might! O my honour! If you refuse, then who shall I hope for by my rebellion?

O brother! Leap then to the door of your Master with high *himma* (yearning) and realize your slaveness! His resplendent lights will shine on you as the Shaykh (Abu Madyan) pointed out with his word, may Allah be pleased with him![15]

The twentieth-century Shaykh Ahmad al-Alawi described the vision his master Sidi Muhammad al-Buzidi, a Shaykh of the Darqawi-Shadhili Order of Sufis received of Abu Madyan:

Our Master, Sidi Muhammad al-Buzidi, was always urging us to visit the tomb of Shaikh Shu'aib Madyan of Tlemcen. He spoke of him with great reverence and said that prayers made at his tomb were answered; and he used to tell us: 'It was through his blessing and with his permission that I went to Morocco. I spent a night at his shrine, and after I had recited some of the Qur'an I went to sleep, and he came to me with one of my ancestors. They greeted me, and then he said: "Go to Morocco. I have smoothed the way for thee." I said: "But Morocco is full of poisonous snakes. I cannot live there." Then he passed his blessed hand over my body and said: "Go and fear not. I will protect thee from any mishap that might befall thee." I woke up trembling with awe, and immediately on leaving his shrine I turned my face westwards, and it was in Morocco that I met Shaykh Sidi Muhammad ibn Qaddur.'[16]

Abu Madyan brought to North Africa a Spanish form of Sufism later articulated in the works of Ibn 'Arabi integrating ascetic mysticism and the study of Islamic law and the *ad-Hadith*.

15. *Self Knowledge: Commentaries on Sufic Songs* (Norfolk: Diwan Press, 1978).
16. Martin Lings, *A Sufi Saint on the 20th Century* (Berkeley: University of California Press, 1971), pp 59–60.

Abu Madyan had many disciples, some destined to become famous teachers themselves, among them directly, Ibn Sid Bono and indirectly, Shadhili. He transmitted to them the legendary history of al-Hallaj titled *Akhbar al-Hallaj*, which includes Hallaj's infamous study of Iblis (shaytan) titled 'Ta Sin al-Azal'.[17]

Ibn Arabi relates in the *Futuhat* that many people seeking Abu Madyan's *barakat* (blessing) used to kiss the Shaykh's hand. At one time he was asked if this practice had any effect on his *nafs* (ego) to which he replied,

Does the black stone in Mecca find any trace of itself which might take it away from its stoneliness, even though apostles, prophets, and saints continually kiss it?

When his questioners replied in the negative Abu Madyan said,

Well, I am that black stone and carry its authority.

In another source, Henry Corbin's *Imagination in the Sufism of Ibn 'Arabi*, on page 367, we read,

when Abu Madyan was asked if the black stone felt any effect produced upon it by the people who touched it and kissed it, he replied: 'I am the Black stone.'

In his book *Masters of the Path-A History of the Masters of the Nimat-ullahi Sufi Order*, previously mentioned, Dr. Javad Nurbakhsh, the current Master of the Nimatullahi Order, relates in the section on Abu Madyan following the anecdote above that in the vocabulary of the Sufis, the 'black stone' refers to the station of 'effacement of every sign other than God.'[18]

In volume three of Dr. Nurbakhsh's encyclopedic work *Sufi Symbolism* it is related that the Prophet said, 'The Black Stone (the Kaaba) is the right side of God', quoting the passage, 'So turn your face towards it. . . .' (Qur'an II :144).[19]

Tradition tells us that the Holy Stone was brought to Abraham

17. Massignon, *Passion*, vol. 2, p327.
18. Nurbakhsh, *Masters of the Path*, p36.
19. Nurbakhsh, *Sufi Symbolism*, vol. 3, p99.

by an angel from a nearby hill (Abu Qubays) where it had been preserved since reaching the earth from its heavenly origin.

In a *hadith* of the Prophet,

It descended from Paradise whiter that milk, but the sins of the sons of Adam made it black.

Although the 'sons of Adam' may be interpreted to include all of humankind, indeed the immediate sons are Cain, a name which means 'draw to itself,' implying a selfish nature, while Abel can be interpreted as 'breath,' the animating breath of God which is selfishly desired by the material nature and is essential to its *being*. These spiritual children of the union of man (fire) and woman (water) initially become earth and mist (or air, merciful rain, grace), in perfect balance, the 'Philosopher's *Stone*' which is

living, fluxible, clear, nitid, *white as snow*, hot, humid, airy, vaporous and digestive

PHILALETHES

The earthy, material side of Cain 'self-ishly' desires what he sees in his brother Abel's airy spiritual nature, 'the Self.' Cain kills Abel, and as a result, the Holy Stone is fixed in the material world and becomes black. In al-Kimia the latter is simply absorbed by the former resulting in all material phenomena.

The overwhelming spiritual nature of a mediating body, a *qutb* such as Abu Madyan, initiates once again the whitening of the Stone, after the material nature in whoever comes across the *qutb* passes through the dark night of the soul, a living death of the self-ish-ness that is darker than darkness, the black of blacks. This *nigredo* phase in al-Kimia produces then a starry phase, the mirror of the celestial, the whiteness appears, and the final resolution and reunion identified with the Spirit or the Self is achieved. One then becomes as solid and unshakable as a stone.

In another tradition the Kaaba is said to have been built of celestial *rubies* signifying the red sulphur, the transmuting powder or Stone that evolves the base into the golden, or spiritual nature. Alchemically the colors change from black (the prima materia) to white (signifying calcination) to red, or gold (the projection). In this sense the perfection, of course, originates in heaven and descends to earth as a red ruby, from which God's original temple is built. Due to the proximity of the material (earthy nature of mankind) in time it turns white, then black, reversing the alchemical process. It is then left up to the *art* of the alchemist to *initiate* the process of return or *tawba*. Perhaps if Abu Madyan indeed possessed the transforming power *as the Stone*, it follows that his student Ibn 'Arabi was able to become, through the grace of the shaykh, the red sulfur, the *kibrit ahmar*, the end of the Work, the Perfect Man of God.

In the *Kitab manzil al-qutb* or 'Book of the Spiritual Dwelling of the Pole', Ibn 'Arabi enumerates the qualities of the *qutb*, or Pole:

> The Pole is both the centre of the circle of the universe, and its circumference. He is the Mirror of God, and the pivot of the world.... God is perpetually epiphanized to him.... He is located in Mecca, whatever place he happens to be in bodily. When a Pole is enthroned at the level of the *qutbiyya*, all beings, animal or vegetable, make a covenant with him.... This explains the story about the man who saw the huge snake that God had placed around Mount Qaf, which encircles the world. The head and the tail of this snake meet. The man greeted the snake, who returned his greeting and then asked him about Shaykh Abu Madyan, who lived at Bijaya in the Maghrib. The man said, 'How do you come to know Abu Madyan?' The snake answered, 'Is there anyone on earth who does not know him?'[20]

Chapter 336 of Ibn 'Arabi's monumental work the *Futuhat al-Makkiya* or 'Revelations at Mecca' is given over entirely to this universal pact of allegiance with the Pole and states that all the spirits (*arwah*) participate in it; each asks the qutb a question inspired by God and receives an answer not previously known.[21]

Mount Qaf is related to that mountain range[22] where it stands as

---

20. Ibn 'Arabi, 'Kitab manzil al-qutb', *Futuhat* II, p19, quoted in Chodkiewicz, *Seal of the Saints*, p95.
21. Ibid.
22. See the present work, Preface and Appendix I, 'An Operation of Ancient al-Kimia: the Tingere & al-Aksir'.

the Center, or Pole, of the universe and is home to the famous Simo-urgh, the mythical bird[23] which leads the other birds to Unity in Farid ud-Din 'Attar's tale, the *Manteq at-Tair* or 'The Conference of the Birds'.

At the top of Mount Qaf, at the apex, we find the highest single point of Divine Infinity. At this point there is said to be an Emerald *stone*, which is also identified as the cosmic Tree of Knowledge, the *Tuba*, of which Muhammad said:

> The Tuba is a tree in Paradise. God planted it with his own hand and breathed His Spirit into it.
>
> AD-HADITH

From this point originates the single most important text to Her-metica and al-Kimia, *The Emerald Tablet* of Hermes Trismegistos;[24] and also the holy book of Islam, al-Qu'ran, as well as all books of inspired revelation.

> The All-Merciful: He taught the Qur'an.
>
> QUR'AN (55:1–2)

In another *hadith* of the Prophet Muhammad, who as we know received the revelation of the Qur'an from Jabriel, the angel of God, we find,

> God wrote the Qur'an upon the Tablet. The first drop of ink was the dot under the letter b which begins Bismi 'Llah. . . .

The Bismi 'Llah is the invocation ('In the Name of God Most Merci-ful, Most Compassionate') at the beginning of the revelation of al-Qur'an. The single dot under the b is symbolic and synonymous with the Divine Apex at the top of Mount Qaf. It is also often iden-tified with the Imam Ali, the founder of both Shi'ism and Sufism.

The snake encircling Mount Qaf refers to Unity and as a hermetic and alchemical symbol relates to the *Ouroboros*, the snake or dragon

---

23. The Simourgh is often identified with the Phoenix, the mythological 'bird' which rises from the *ashes*. See also Appendix I.

24. See the present work, Appendix II, 'The Emerald Tablet Attributed to Her-mes Trismegistos'.

who bites its tail and represents the All, the totality of the Work. In another context among its many other symbolic interpretations, it may also represent the dragon guarding the 'secret' of immortality.[25]

A contemporary of Ibn 'Arabi, Shihabuddin Yahya Suhrawardi, also called al-Maqtul, 'the martyred', was known as the *Shaykh al-Ishraq*, or the 'Master of Illumination'. He died in prison at age thirty-eight in 1191 and was also known by the 'vulgar *ulama*' or the common exoteric Muslim as an alchemist. The label 'alchemist' was also used in a derogatory context to describe Suhrawardi's predecessor al-Hallaj (d. 922),[26] whose theology certainly influenced Suhrawardi and who was also martyred for his 'heretical' teachings.

Suhrawardi resembles *malamatiyya* who give little thought to their appearance in the world, choosing to veil their spiritual station in this way and by other 'deceptive' means. His was the doctrine of the First Light, *an-Nur*, a holy Name of God in Islam found in the revelation of al-Qur'an, which is also for Suhrawardi related to the 'Light' in opposition to 'Darkness' in ancient Mazdean Iran. In his visionary treatises or recitals fashioned after the recitals of Ibn Sina, Suhrawardi uses marvelous symbol and imagery. In the recital titled *'Aql-surkh* or 'The Red Intellect' he encounters a personage whose countenance is *red*. When he asks why he is this color the personage replies that he is a luminous Elder and is really *white*, but that he was thrown into a *black* pit, and when mixed with *black*, every white thing connected to the light appears *red*, like the sun at its setting or after *the dawn*. When asked where he comes from, the personage replies that he resides beyond Mount Qaf, and he tells Suhrawardi, who appears in the recital as a trapped *falcon*, a symbol of the intellect, that *his nest is there too, but he has forgotten it.*[27]

Suhrawardi al-Maqtul received the Hermetic wisdom that animated the thought of Dhu l'Nun, and continued in the same way the traditions of ancient Persia and Egypt.

25. There are myriad symbolic interpretations of the *Ouroboros* as well as the act of slaying the dragon in al-Kimia.

26. See note 17.

27. Suhrawardi, al-Maqtul, *The Mystical and Visionary Treatises of Suhrawardi*, trans. by W.M. Thackson, Jr. (London: Octagon, 1982).

In chapter 45 of the *Futuhat*, Ibn 'Arabi refers to the saints who return (*raji'un*), as those who, having arrived at Unity, return to multiplicity. This return is closely related to the manifestation of God's Mercy (*ar-Rahman*) toward the creation.

Those perfected ones who 'choose' to return at the 'request' of God with the intention of teaching and guiding others enter in to the supreme mode of participation in the heritage of the prophets. In the case of Abu Madyan, according to Ibn' Arabi, this 'choice' to return was spontaneous, in contrast to the return of Abu Yazid al-Bastami, which was divinely commanded. These two examples present another example of classic Sufi opposition, that of sobriety (*sahw*) and drunkenness (*sukr*).[28] When considering the permanent state, or the non-position beyond states and stations, of saints, of course, these categorizations are meaningless in the extreme.

In the words of Abu Madyan contained in the same text:

To flee from created being is one of the signs of a novice's sincerity. To reach God is a sign of the sincerity of his flight from created being. To return to created being is a sign of the sincerity of his having reached God.[29]

Ibn' Arabi points out that the Prophet Muhammad's experience before the revelation of al-Qur'an corresponds to the flight from created being, and his return *with the revelation*, or more precisely, *as* the revelation is for the benefit of all beings. This example of the Prophet's becomes the model for the heirs of this tradition, the saints, who follow him.

The root of the word 'Qur'an' means to gather together and totalization. Abu Madyan said:

The aspirant (*al murid*) is really an aspirant only when he finds in the Qu'ran all to which he aspires. And word not endowed with this plenitude is not really Qur'an.[30]

28. See the present work, chap. 6, 'Hakim Abu-Ali al-Husayn Abd Allah Ibn Sina', on the 'opposition' between '*aql* and *qalb*.

29. Ibn 'Arabi, *Futuhat al-Makiyya*, chap. 45.

30. See al-Hajj Umar, *Kitab ar-Rimah*, vol. 2, pp 4, 5, 16.

According to Ibn 'Arabi,

> It [the revelation of the Qur'an] came down upon the heart of
> Muhammad, and it does not cease to come down upon the
> hearts of the faithful of this community up to the Day of the Res-
> urrection. Its descent upon hearts is always new, for it is perpet-
> ual Revelation.[31]

Everything relating to Islam and specifically to Sufism preceding Ibn
'Arabi was coalesced and restated afresh in his ideas: nothing in the
succeeding field of Sufi thought has escaped the impact of his enor-
mous influence and contribution.

Ibn 'Arabi was the first to synthesize what he received from the
Sufi tradition and from the Greeks, and also from the larger body of
Hermetic knowledge in general.

The majority of his popular works persist in producing comment
and study. Among them we find the *Fusus al-Hikam*, which perhaps
summarizes his entire teaching and the previously mentioned *Futuhat al-Makkiyya*. His writings are accessible to the scholar and lay-
man alike on many simultaneous levels of interpretation.

A possible outgrowth of *jafr* considered in its broader sense may
be found in Ibn 'Arabi's *al-Istilah al-Suffiyyah*, a compilation of Sufi
technical terms which serves to illustrate how its author wishes 'to
reveal the occult.'

In this document listing 199 brief definitions, Ibn 'Arabi apparently intended the material presented to be of immediate usefulness
to students who had no other ready access to general Sufi terminology. One example is his definition of *salik*, a term used above in reference to Abu Madyan's early life:

> Salik: The traveler. The one who traverses the stages by his state,
> not by his knowledge, so that for him knowledge is experience
> (*'ayn*).[32]

---

31. See ash-Shar'ani, *Al-Yawaqit wa l'jawahir*, Cairo, 1360 AH.

32. See 'Sufi Terminology-Ibn 'Arabi's al-Istilah al-Sufiyyah', trans. by Rabia
Terri Harris in *The Journal of the Muhiyiddin Ibn 'Arabi Society*, vol. III, Oxford,
1984, pp 27–54.

It is easy to see that this is a far more satisfactory and instructive definition for the term *salik*, which is usually defined as simply, *a wayfarer on the path*. In terms of al-Kimia, Ibn 'Arabi's definition of *salik* bears close resemblance with the alchemist who must confirm knowledge by application,

> When then the consideration of everything has been rightly undertaken, which, as mentioned before, is nothing but Theoria, it is followed by the right, true preparation, which preparation must be done through manual work, so that something factual and real may follow afterward.
>
> BASILIUS VALENTINUS

The inclusion of 'ayn (eye) at the end of the phrase can be attributed to the saying 'seeing is believing'.

In a more specific and unique application of the broader implications of *jafr*, Ibn 'Arabi looks closely at the roots of words of the Arabic language as it specifically applies to the vocabulary of revelation in al-Qur'an. In a reversal of exoteric application and reading, he reveals that certain root letters, words, and whole phrases which appear to say in a literal sense that something, an act, or someone is *blameworthy*, for example, have an opposite reading, implying that the literal words hide other meanings, other levels of understanding. This idea applies to Hermetic lore in general, which, when passed on by everyone in the form of tales, legends, and stories is kept alive for future adepts who can reveal other levels beneath the surface.

Ibn 'Arabi was familiar with the legacy and no doubt used its precedent in the formulation of his study of the Qur'an. He calls those who can use his system (or any system) of *jafr* the *sahirun* or magicians[33] who God has bestowed with the science of the letters. Using the root of the word *kafirun, kfr*, which means 'to hide', he thus describes the highest level of the *malamatiyya*, the 'people of blame', mentioned repeatedly in this study, who are God's saints and *hide* under the traits of His enemies, as the literal explanation of those known as *kafirun, kufr*, etc. in al-Qur'an is generally accepted.

---

33. The root of the word 'magician' is 'magi', referring to the adepts of ancient Persia.

His doctrine of the Perfect Man, as the quintessence of the spiritual possibilities of this material world, defines, or rather refines, the notion popular across religious boundaries of the role of the realized person as vice-regent of God.[34]

In another short work by Ibn 'Arabi translated by Henry Corbin in his alchemically titled collection: *Spiritual Body and Celestial Earth: From Mazdean Iran to Shi'ite Iran* called 'The Earth Which Was Created From What Remained of the Clay of Adam',[35] Adam is identified as the first Imam, and Eve his feminine Imam counterpart. In the *imaginal* realm described, mystics must leave behind their earthly, fleshly form and enter in a body possessing the same spiritual quality as the spirit world they aspire to inhabit. Everyone the mystic meets above has like himself a corresponding fleshly reality below where the ascent began, the Earth previously mentioned in the title.

According to Suhrawardi al-Maqtul, the soul has a previous dwelling in the angelic realm. When it comes into existence as a human being, the soul divides into two parts, one part remaining in heaven and the other part dwelling in the Earth of the body.

The act of prayer effects a return to an origin from which the person praying must return while dwelling in this earthly adobe. This relationship of prayer is one built on *tawba*, repentance, or return to one's Lord, in which prayer activates a reciprocal mode based on necessity and union and the attribute that shines above and through all the others, a Qur'anic name of God: *Rahman*, or the divine Mercy, of which God says in the Qur'an (7:156):

My Mercy (Rahman) encompasseth all things. . . .

and (41:54):

Surely He encompasses everything.

and (25:6):

---

34. See 'The Perfect Man', in R.A. Nicholson's *Studies in Islamic Mysticism* (Cambridge: Cambridge University Press, 1921).

35. Henry Corbin, *Spiritual Body and Celestial Earth: From Mazdean Iran to Shi'ite Iran* (Princeton: Princeton University Press, 1977), p135.

Prostrate yourselves to the All-Merciful.

Where does one who prays to his Lord *with every breath* dwell at any given point in time or space? On many levels at once, apparently, and *nowhere* in particular: as above, so below.

Wherever you turn, there is the Face of God.

QUR'AN (2:115)

The Earth left over in the creation of Adam and by association, Eve, Ibn 'Arabi describes as about the size of a sesame seed. In a *hadith qudsi*, God announces:

> My heavens and My earth embrace Me not, but the heart of My believing servant does embrace Me.

The heart, then, is the psycho-spiritual loci of the Divine, the inmost dwelling place of sanctity within the Earth of the physical body of the believer, which moves through space constantly without an exact location and yet remains in close proximity to the *heart of the matter* at any given time. Mansur al-Hallaj in his work *The Tawasin*, says:

> I saw my Lord with the eye of my heart
> I said: 'Who are you?' He said: 'You!'
> But for You, 'where' cannot have a place
> And there is no 'where' when it concerns You.
> The mind has no image of your existence in time
> Which would permit the mind to know where you are.
> You are the one who encompasses every 'where'
> Up to the point of no-where
> So where are you?[36]

Ibn 'Arabi's works are colored red with al-Kimia, and the analogous role it plays in the entire transmutative process of human realization is articulated in terms unique to his viewpoint originating with the holy revelation of al-Qur'an.

In al-Kimia, or simply put, *in life*, each moment brings transformation and *change* with every inhalation and exhalation.

---

36. Mansur al-Hallaj, *The Tawasin* (London: Diwan, 1974).

Symbolically, and as this life defines symbol, the pure spirit needs the body in order to *materialize the spirit* and the body must die in one sense or another, as the Prophet said:

Ye must die before ye die.

Again and again and again. A transmutation is required to effect the *spiritualization of matter*. Whenever living beings disappear, they leave behind a subtle essence, or 'body', which in esoteric Islam is called the *jism mithali*. *Solve et coagula*, dissolve and coalesce, in other words, 'to make of the body a spirit and of the spirit a body.' This is the basis of al-Kimia, nothing more simple can define the term. One and one do not make two, the One divides and multiplies, yet remains One. There is nothing lost by dying; spirit and matter constantly transmute in form and formlessness.

It is small wonder that prayers are answered at the tombs of the righteous, where the bodies of saints produce the seeds of resurrection, for without the creation and *art* of the perfected Nature, nothing returns, nothing creates, nothing cannot even *be nothing*.

For Ibn 'Arabi, whose most beloved teacher Abu Madyan was identified as being the *stone*, the continual revelation of God's word is a living, breathing creation. Those highest saints, who are known as the *malamatiyya*, the blameworthy of this world, the 'hidden' or *kafirun* of God are the embodiment of all the systems of concealment and disclosure, *jafr, ta'wil, taqqiyah*, et al. The Qur'an is not just a book, it is a *person*. The texts of al-Kimia are not simple words which when put together produce magical formulas, they are *alive*.

Let him forbear who believes that Alchemy is concerned solely with the mundane, mineral and metallic nature of things.

Let him forbear, who believes that Alchemy is purely spiritual.

But those who understand that Alchemy is but a symbol used to reveal by analogy the process of achieving 'Spiritual Realization'- in a word, that man is at once the prime matter and the anthanor of the Work-let them pursue it with all their might.'

CLAUDE D'YGE
New Assembly of Chymical Philosophers

'We shall show them Our signs upon the horizons and in themselves, until it is clear to them that He is the Real.'

QUR'AN (41:53)

9

AL-KIMIA:
THE SACRED ART

This gold is our male, and it is sexually joined to a more crude white gold-the female seed: the two together being indissolubly united, constitute our fruitful Hermaphrodite.

PHILALETHES

IT IS COMMON WHEN READING ALCHEMICAL TEXTS for the reader to observe consistent references to the practice of al-Kimia as 'our art', 'this art', or 'the art' or descriptions of the way to accomplish an alchemical process: 'by art' or 'with art.' This use of the term art refers to the alchemist's understanding not only of the concepts and theories of all the Arts, but also implies the plastic applications involved in undertaking any actual *work* of art.

This is the *Ars Magna* in which there is no context concerning the word *art* that cannot be applied also to the whole concept of Alchemy. The Arts considered in the present tense have become specialized and separated into arbitrary categories; whereas the art of al-Kimia, encompassing all of these categories and beyond, has remained all-inclusive.

What follows is a brief discussion on the subject of color, followed by an equally cursory glance at some of the arts of antiquity and their apparent relationships with al-Kimia and esoteric Islam. The correspondences drawn are at times broad; it should become obvious that this subject generally deserves more time and space than is possible in the present study.

With some variation the primary colors usually correspond to the

four active elements found in al-Kimia: Fire/Red, Air/Yellow, Water/
Green, and Earth/Blue. Fire is hot and dry, Air is hot and wet, Water
is cold and wet, Earth is cold and dry.

The *Resala-ye lama'at was resala-ye estelahat* of 'Iraqi edited by Dr.
Javad Nurbakhsh states:

> Redness represents strength in the traveling of the Path. Yellow-
> ness is said to represent weakness in the traveling of the Path.
> Blueness is said to represent the blending of loving-kindness
> (mahabbat) with whatever is other than loving-kindness. Green-
> ness represents absolute perfection.[1]

An alchemical marriage closely related to that of the quaternary of
the elements Fire, Air, Water, and Earth, and the principal ternary
Sulphur, Mercury, and Salt is performed by adding the group of four
primaries representing Nature to another three that relate to Spirit:
usually white, black, and orange (or sandalwood), and assigning
these seven colors to the planets that rule each day of the week.

In classical alchemical terminology, the *Nigredo* or black stage of
the alchemical work is generally associated with putrefaction. The
Albedo or white stage is most often associated with a step in the calcination process although it may obviously have other connotations
as well. The *Rubedo* stage represents the formation of the Red Solar
Stone or the Red Sulphur, the *kibrit al-ahmar.*

It is interesting that with few exceptions, the Sun is identified with
the male and the Moon with the female.[2] In the symbolism of al-
Kimia the former represents sulphur and the later mercury. When
these two are joined in marriage, the *Coniunctio* is achieved, the
spiritualization of the material. The Sun is symbolic of the Light of
God, which reflects brightly upon the Moon, symbolized by the
heart or *qalb* in Sufism. The mirror heart of the mystic manifests
and embodies the light or *Nur* of the Divine.

---

1. 'Iraqi, *Resala-ye lama'at was resala-ye estelahat,* ed. by Dr. Javad Nurbakhsh,
Tehran, 1974. See also the 12 volume encyclopedia *Sufi Symbolism* by Dr. Javad Nurbakhsh for a comprehensive examination of the science of Sufi symbolism.

2. However, depending on a particular culture and time period, this is not
always the case. See 'The Marriage of Sun and Moon', by Arthur Versluis in *Avaloka:
A Journal of Traditional Religion and Culture',* vol. iv, nos. 1 & 2, pp30–39.

Isaac Newton, that oft forgotten practitioner of Alchemy, in 1666 found that when white light passed through a prism, it divided into bands of color that appeared to make up the visible spectrum. This led to the theory of color as light vibrating at different wavelengths, which when combined produce a white light. Johann Wolfgang von Goethe, and William Blake both considered this Newtonian spectrum of colors to be an illusory 'spectre'. Goethe devoted an entire book to the subject, entitled the *History of Colour Theory* (1810). Newton's work undoubtedly inspired him to produce his own theories, and Goethe is generally seen aligning himself more with the ideas connected with Hermeticism, concluding that colors are originally derived not only from light, but from a mixture of darkness as well. Blake felt that the triumph of the visionary over the physical existence of phenomena was heralded by the appearance of the rainbow symbolizing (in his mythos) the harmony of the four elementary creatures (Zoas) over and above the dark ocean of time and space.

Henry Corbin, in his essay 'The Realism and Symbolism of Colours in Shi'ite Cosmology' found in the book of his collected essays entitled *Temple and Contemplation*,[3] describes the color theory of the Shi'ite alchemist Shaykh Muhammad Karim-Khan Kirmani (d. 1870). In this Shaykh's Neoplatonic view, color exists as a self-existent entity, or archetype. All 'archetypes' can be considered to proceed from the One source, and they exist *potentially* in this union and therefore 'exist' before they are manifested as colors discernible to our physical eyes. Perhaps from the point of view of Unity these theories have more in common than what initially 'meets the eye'?

In Corbin's *The Man of Light in Iranian Sufism*,[4] he examines the work of another alchemist, the Sufi master and founder of the Kobrawiyya Order, Abo'l-Jannab Najmo'd-Din ibn 'Omar al-Kobra (b. AD 1145). Kobra formulated a theory based on *tajalli* or theophany, wherein a person becomes a receptacle for divine perceptions

---

3. See Henry Corbin, *Temple and Contemplation* (London: KPI, 1986), chap. 1.
4. See Henry Corbin, *The Man of Light in Iranian Sufism* (Boulder: Shambala, 1978).

by specifically developing the sensory and supersensory organs of perception.

Another work on Kobra edited by F. Meier titled *Fawaih al-gamal wa fawatih al-galal*, states Kobra's description of this theory in action:

> When you see before you a vast expanse opening out toward the distance, there is clear air above you and you see on the far horizon colors such as green, red, yellow, and blue, know that you are going to pass through that air to where those colors are. The colors pertain to spiritual states. Green is the sign of life of the heart (this being the highest state). The color of pure fire indicates the life of 'spiritual concentration' (himma), which denotes power (of actualization). If this fire be dark, that betokens the fire of exertion and shows the seeker to be weary and afflicted after the battle with the lower ego and the Devil. Blue is the color of the life of the ego. Yellow is the color of lassitude. All these are suprasensory realities that speak with him who experiences them in the two languages of inner tasting (dhawq) and visionary apperception. These are two reliable, mutual corroboratory witnesses: what you behold with inner vision you also experience within yourself, and what you experience inwardly you also behold with inner vision.[5]

When the Man of Light approaches the color green, he sees a circular Sun-like countenance, which Kobra recognizes:

> This face is, in reality, your own face and this sun is the Sun of the Spirit which oscillates within your body. Then your entire body is immersed in purity, and at that moment you see before you a person made of light, who generates light. The spiritual traveler, too, then experiences his entire body as generating light. It may be that the veil will fall from all individuality, so that you see totality through the totality of your body. The faculty of inner vision is opened first in the eyes, then the face, then the breast, then in the whole body. This person of light in front of

5. See F. Meier, *Fawaih al-gamal wa fawatih al-galal*, 1963.

you is called by the People (Sufis) the 'Suprasensory Guide,' and is also known as the 'Suprasensory (Personal) Master' or the 'Suprasensory Scales (of Judgement)'.[6]

The unity of the warp and the weave of the beautifully designed carpets of the Middle East make use of the color theory much in the same way that Persian miniatures are conceived and produced. The art of dyeing fabric utilizes a process of tincturing the color from plants and other substances and this operation stands as one of the original alchemical manipulations of Nature.

In general, Islamic artwork denies the human physical form in favor of the geometric. Stylized flora and other creaturely forms derived from Nature are, however, often considered acceptable and not in danger of 'idolization'. Much has been written on the esoteric arts of Islam including decorative architecture, miniature painting, and book illumination, all of which at times incorporate elaborate calligraphy and the *arabesque*.

The unique exceptional beauty of the Persian miniature is usually found accompanying historical text or poetry. The letters written by al-Hallaj were said to have been illuminated and colored upon precious material. Manichaean illuminated holy books, as well as early Christian iconography, also belong to this tradition: we should remember that 'Catacomb' Christianity operated under occultation and the punishment of death.

Tradition tells us that when Muhammad ordered the removal of all idols from the holy Kaaba, the original temple believed to have been built by Abraham in Mecca, the inside walls were covered with paintings of pagan deities also destined to be painted over. Muhammad placed his hands over an icon of the Virgin Mary and the child Jesus and also a tiny painting presumed to be of Abraham. These were spared the blank painted overlay.

Two authors, often identified with the Traditional school, S.H. Nasr and Titus Burckhardt have written many works on the subject of Islamic art including the former's *Islamic Art and Spirituality*, and *Knowledge and the Sacred*; and the latter's *Mirror of the Intellect*, and

---

6. Ibid., pp31–32.

Sacred Art in East and West.[7] These distinguished scholars have each treated at length the importance of the Void in Islamic art, sometimes considered as 'negative' space in the West.[8]

The Void, which is at once dynamic and stable, is the perfect model for the ground of all being, the place wherefrom all things proceed and recede (or re-seed) in Absolute Unity. The Void is related to both *fana* (annihilation) and *baqa* (subsistence) in Sufism, and the path of *via negativa* in Christianity. It is the silence of the sages, the blank tablet awaiting revelation. It is represented by the 'whiteness' of which 'Iraqi says:

[Whiteness] represents the integrity achieved through complete attention to God and severance from what is other than God.[9]

The Void then, considered 'hidden treasure,' wishes to be revealed by imagery, cipher, and symbol; in a *conscious form.*

I was a hidden treasure and I loved to be known, so I created the world so that I might be known.

HADITH QUDSI

The alchemist is the consummate artist who reveals God to Himself by ultimately acting as a *nabi*, a prophet sent to himself from Himself. By *anamnesis* or self-remembering his Divine origin, he recalls and activates this cosmic presence and purpose. He is a spiritual evolutionist working on, at least, the physical plane.

Thoth-Hermes (Mercury) traditionally is considered to be the intermediary or originator of all language, of all arts and sciences, all alphabets, in short, the angel or god-like messenger of all symbolic knowledge emanating from God. An alchemist is the one who reveals by *art* the Hermetic identity realized by remembrance, or *zikr*, the Word, or Name of God.

In their texts, Islamic alchemists rarely depend on symbol beyond

7. See present work, Bibliography.

8. See Nasr's essay 'The Significance of the Void in Islamic Art' and also Burckhardt's essay 'The Void in Islamic Art'. Of course, the Void would be embraced by Abstract Expressionism, especially, for example, in the work (and life) of Mark Rothko.

9. See first section of note 1.

what is found naturally occurring in revelatory language. The practice of using secret symbols and alphabets, however, abounds in the alchemical texts found in Europe in the Middle Ages. The origins of these practices may be traced directly to early Egyptian Hermeticism, and consequently to later exegetical Qu'ranic systems such as *jafr*.

In the middle period in European history, alchemical art most often takes the form of engravings, emblems, and paintings frequently incorporated within illuminated texts. Contemporary scholar Stanislas Klossowski de Rola has accomplished much in renewing interest in these arts with his books *The Golden Game: Alchemical Engravings of the Seventeenth Century*, and *Alchemy: the Secret Art*. Adam McLean's work in this vein is also worthy of note. His entire *Magnum Opus Hermetic Sourceworks* series is highly recommended.

Perhaps the doctrinal non-human-formal rigidity of the arts of Islam forced the hand of artistic total abstraction, based in greater part on a geometry in which a continually diminishing variable approaches zero as its limit, the Void.

What comes out of the 'Void from which all things proceed' in the general world of abstract figurative arts must remain the subject of large, unwieldy art history tomes, however, it is necessary to examine a few broadly related abstract forms and attempt to attribute at least part of their symbolic significance to al-Kimia, the Sacred Art.

The *Ishtar Gate* from Babylon, Iraq (c. 575 BC) was one of the eight gates leading into the city of Babylon, where Nebuchadnezzar built his palace complete with the *ziggurat* considered to have been the Biblical Tower of Babel.

The gate, which has been restored and installed in the Vorderasiatisches Museum in Berlin, is faced with beautiful glazed brick in a background of royal blue with geometric ornamentation in white and gold. Widely spaced stylized bulls and dragons in raised relief are composed of several separately molded and glazed bricks.

According to Babylonian tradition, the goddess Ishtar, identified with the planet Venus governing both love and war, descended to Hades to obtain the *water of life* in order to restore to life the dead Thammuz. Thammuz is described as dwelling in the midst of a great tree at the center of the earth. The description of the Divine One who descends, the reference to calcination (Hades), and the *return* with the elixir (the water of life) for the dead one resurrected to life at the point of the divine center, the tree of knowledge which may be identified as the *Tuba*, evokes a striking alchemical allegory.

The *arabesque* and the geometrical intricacy of Islamic art has its spiritual/material antecedent in the weaver's loom and is related to the Animal Style of the 'Barbaric' European nomads. The Animal Style influenced the illuminated complexity of some Hiberno-Saxon art, especially in illuminated gospels such as the Irish *Book of Kells* (c. AD 760–820). The hide and seek aspect of this artistic development has affinity with the Islamic Void from which exegesis, and for that matter its opposite, concealment, proceeds. Again, a point of reference may be the use of *jafr* in the interpretation of al-Qur'an, however; the concept of a divinity that is hidden and also at times revealed is complex and indeed *the original model*.

The search for the origins of the highly abstract and so-called monstrous symbolic bestiaries of the illustrated alchemical texts of Medieval Europe may begin where the art of al-Kimia as we know it began, in ancient *Kem* (Egypt).

In *Kem* a pre-logical hieroglyphic picture script carries a series of meaningful correspondences in *silence* with alchemical emblem texts, such as the *Mutus Liber* by Altus (1677).[10] When an attempt is made to decipher this silent correspondence we are inevitably confronted with the larger mystery of our own symbolic existence. When reason is confounded in this way a void appears which may precipitate revelation.

The contemporary West places emphasis upon literal meaning in the interpretation of two-dimensional and three-dimensional art. According to this viewpoint Art must ultimately exist by explanation only, and this process is defined absolutely by the choice and the arrangement of language. If the explanation is satisfactory, then another confident explanation follows that attempts to resolve what the work of art might 'mean.' In the end, this art criticism only serves

10. See Adam McLean, *A Commentary on the Mutus Liber* (Grand Rapids: Phanes, 1991).

to perpetuate itself by verbal expression, an oral and consequentially literal supposition of meaning in which symbol refers to symbol and serves language and logic but by no means brings about a complete understanding (which must include a 'non-understanding') of the artwork. Of course, everyone is entitled to their own opinions.

What stands under the surface, at the same time it exists on the surface for the organs of perception, is essentially a non-verbal experience, a silent recognition by spirit of symbol. The act of looking then becomes a means to activate a form of spiritual participation in which subject and object become One. In this perception in which the external experience joins with the internal consciousness is found pure *form* devoid of the processes of verbal expression, memory, and even creative imagination. To participate with image it is not a simple matter of the visual contemplation of the object, but also a search for the artist, the gesture of the hand, the thought behind the gesture, the alchemical process of looking and transforming Nature into Art.

Students of revelatory texts, including all good alchemical texts, do well to slowly savor even the image of a single word and to look at the text again and again at different intervals of time to gain the basic intent of the artist/author, the gesture of grace, which is only relevant to the *present moment*.

A single cup is sufficient to reveal the flavor of a wine, and a single word from a *hesychast* can reveal to those with taste his whole inner condition and activity.[11]

JOHN CLIMACUS

Of course, hieroglyphics often accompany larger paintings as a running pictographic text, and to carry on the initial comparison, certainly most alchemical engravings are found in text books. Consider Michael Maier's (1568–1622) remarkable *Atalanta Fugiens*,[12] which

11. St. John Climacus, *The Ladder of Divine Ascent* (Ramsey: Paulist Press, 1982), p 273. A hesychast is one who is master of the 'prayer of the heart' or the 'Jesus prayer' which transmutates the inner being of the Christian practitioner much in the same way as the *zikr* in Sufism, or the Hindu *mantra*.

12. See present work, Bibliography.

combines fifty outstanding engravings and fifty accompanying epigrams in Latin coupled with their translation in German verse with
fifty fugues musically corresponding to the artwork and the text!

With the incredible bias of the English language ill-fitted to a
scarcely glimpsed and much less understood (since the deciphering
of the Rosetta Stone in 1821) Egyptian world-view based on *formal*
intuition, now let us, like so many amateur Egyptologists, forge
ahead blindly through the corridors of time and space to the image
of the Sphinx, that most ancient and silent of sages, who, as Fulcanelli says of Nature generally:

> . . . . does not open the door of the sanctuary indiscriminately to
> everyone.[13]

The Sphinx, a hybrid of a man and beast shall be the symbol, the
model for this next step of our study. This monumental sculpture,
inscrutable and still as *stone*, was and presumably remains a central
symbol of *Kem*, or part of a 'text' of al-Kimia which can be deci-
phered and read by adepts much like the sculpture and architecture
of the French cathedrals examined by Fulcanelli.[14] Tehuti or Thoth,
the figure associated with Hermes in ancient Egypt, is himself
depicted as a hieroglyphic Ibis-headed hybrid.

Certainly the Pyramids are early al-Kimical symbols culminating
in the point of divine origin,[15] then proceeding downward like the
rays of the Sun (*Ra: considered the One, self-existent God*) in the
expansive gesture of the Divine Mercy (*ar-Rahman*). The symbol of
the triangle is synonymous with sulphur, or Sol, the Sun, which
ancient Egyptians believed was coalesced in the earth as metallic gold.

The *ziggurats* of early Mesopotamia served a different and yet
similar function as artificial mountains, high places designed for ritual worship in which proximity encouraged the union of participant
and deity.

---

13. Mary Sworder, *Fulcanelli Master Alchemist: Esoteric Interpretation of the
Hermetic Symbols of the Great Work*, a translation of Fulcanelli's *Le Mystère des
Cathedrales* (Albuquerque: Brotherhood of Life, 1984), p175.

14. Ibid.

15. See present work, chap. 8, 'Shu'ayb ibn al-Husayn al'Ansari Abu Madyan',
for the symbolism of Mount Qaf; and see also the Preface.

The *idea* as a *form*, as a messenger of God flying from the Void to the Earth may be considered in the traditional concept of an angel. Birds are also traditional symbolic intermediaries between the material and spiritual worlds. The union of the idea of bird with angel in Mazdean Iran becomes, in later usage, an emblem of the Holy Spirit.[16]

At the gate of the Palace of King Sargon II (Assyrian, eighth century) at Dur Sharrukin (Khorsabad), are found large relief sculptures of lion-like beings with the bodies of bulls, diagonally elevated wings, and human heads with long curly beards and many-tiered divine headdresses. Compare these wonderful and fantastic beings with the image found in a version of the *Ripley Scrowle* drawn by James Standysh in the sixteenth century on page 96 of Stanislaw de Rola's *Alchemy: The Secret Art*, which bears a caption that begins: 'The bird of Hermes is my name....'

The 'Night Journey', or *Mi'raj*; the ascension of Muhammad to the 'Lote tree of the uttermost limit', the nearest proximity allowed to being in the presence of God, was accomplished by his riding a fantastic horse-like being with wings called *al-Buraq*. This mount was supplied to the Prophet by the Archangel Jabriel. In India, *al-Buraq* is depicted with the face of a woman and the tail of a peacock and had been described as being symbolic of the intellect. The peacock is also an alchemical symbol for the multiple color changes expected to occur during the purification of the base material.

River deities and other 'monsters of the imagination' found throughout antiquity are subtle links between the spiritual and material. In Greek mythology the *Chimera* is a fire-breathing monster with a lion's head, a goat's body, and a serpent's tail. It is said that the Sphinx, and the Nemean Lion, which Heracles killed as his first labor, were the offspring of the Chimera and Orthos, a two-headed dog killed by Heracles in the course of completing his tenth labor.

Pan, the god of pandemonium, panic, and pantheism was the offspring of Hermes and Dryope, a nymph of Lemnos who was changed into a tree; she is also associated with a wondrous fountain

16. For the related symbols of the Phoenix and Simourgh see chap. 8, note 23, and text.

known as Pegae. Pan is described as a being part-man and part-goat, credited with the invention of the flute with seven reeds, signifying the seven planetary spheres. The name Pan, of course, signifies the *All*, and his domain is at once universal and particularly identified with Nature in the wild. His sun-like face, and upturned horns representing the traditional symbol of the moon, remind one of the Crescent (moon) and Star (sun), the central symbol(s) of Islam. The embodiment of symbolism found in Pan makes him the perfect image of the philosophic Mercury, which is at once solar and lunar. For a wonderful representation of this syncretic god, see the illustration by an anonymous artist of the 14th century reproduced on page 75 of *Alchemy*: *The Secret Art* by Stanislas Klossowski de Rola.

Gargoyles in Medieval cathedrals have often been thought of as reminders of Hyle or Chaos, and the presence of the irrational as the basis or intrinsic element of an otherwise reasonable order.

The lofty position of these hybrids on the tops of the cathedrals Fulcanelli defines as virtual textbooks of Alchemy, however, suggests that they also may symbolize steps in the process or even the completion of the Work, the new thing, the marriage of opposites which spiritually transforms Nature and resolves all conflict, all duality. In his masterwork *Le Mystere des Cathedrales*,[17] Fulcanelli identifies a figure in stone as The Alchemist in the vicinity of the highest part of the main axis of the North tower of the cathedral of Notre Dame in Paris. On page 14 of the book entitled *Notre Dame de Paris*[18] is found a photo with a broader angle than the plate containing Fulcanelli's Alchemist in *Le Mystere des Cathedrales*. In this photo we see that The Alchemist is situated next to the sculpture of a curious Gargoyle with the head of a dog or lion and the claws of an eagle, with a muscular human frame and prominent feminine breasts.

Plate two of a group of four plates from Steffan Michelspacher's *Cabala, Speigel der Kunst und Nature*, (Augsburg, 1616) contains a hybrid beast with three feminine udders which also bears the characteristics of the Four Holy Living Creatures: the Bull's horns, the Man's face, the Lion's body, and the Eagle's talons.

---

17. See note 13 above, plate between pages 72 and 73.
18. Richard Winston, 'Notre Dame de Paris', *Newsweek*, New York, 1971.

In the text attributed to Hermes Trismegistos entitled *The Poimondres*,[19] there are several references to the bisexuality of God and the sacred androgynous nature in which mind (*nous*) is male and substantive, while thought (*epinoia and ennoia*) as process, is considered female. The conjunction of the two sexes becomes a sacrament of the heavenly love found in all beings, indeed, found in all of creation.

Paracelsus defined Rebis as a bisexual thing combining the two antitheses in the highest and most desirable degree of the process of transmutation-totality.

Fulcanelli refers to Rebis as

> a double matter, at once both dry and humid, the amalgam of philosophic gold and mercury, a combination which has received a double occult property, exactly equilibrated, from nature and from art.[20]

The alchemical marriage of philosophical sulphur and mercury, sun and moon, as a central symbol of Alchemy is often depicted in paintings found in later European texts as a two-headed human being with the sexual apparatus of both male and female. This is the symbol, the culmination of the union of opposites in coitus, the compelling force at work in the universe, Eros.

Concerning the *eroticism* which mixes the forces of death and life in a sensual form of the creative act crystallized in the image of the androgyne, or *hermaphrodite*, a term derived from the joining of Hermaphroditos, the son of Hermes and Aphrodite, the goddess of Love, with the body of the nymph Salmacis, George Bataille notes:

> It is the common business of sacrifice to bring life and death into harmony, to give death the upsurge of life, life the momentousness and the vertigo of death opening on to the unknown. Here life is mingled with death, but simultaneously death is a sign of life.[21]

19. Hermes Trismegistos, *Corpus Hermeticum*, 'Libellus'.

20. See note 13 above, p160.

21. George Bataille, *Erotism: Death and Sensuality* (San Francisco: City Lights., 1986), p91.

This sacrifice of a most intimate aspect of presumed individuality for the sake of the creation of the truly individual perfected nature is the holy art and union of life wherein each part is invited to participate and join with the whole in the unity that denies all opposition.

The *art* of al-Kimia is nothing if not an articulation and manipulation of this basic and naturally sacred process.

APPENDIX I

AN OPERATION OF ANCIENT AL-KIMIA:
THE TINGERE AND AL-AKSIR

THE TERM *tingere* or 'tincture', to 'tinge', may originally have meant to color, or to draw the color from a plant or other substance by means of immersion in a liquid. The art of dyeing fabric then finds it origin within al-Kimia, and continues to be an important aspect of our daily lives. Drawing the essence from a substance with a liquid for human consumption is equally related and also affects our lives in such ubiquitous acts as making a pot of coffee or a cup of tea. Cooking food is a basic transmutative act and taken back a step to gardening, in which the gardener is an integral part of a natural action that produces a plant for cultivation, it may be seen how closely the art of living with and as a part of the Earth's natural rhythms is connected to the art of al-Kimia. In fact, the basic functions of the human body are *the* model of al-Kimical operations.

A chickpea leaps almost over the rim of the pot
where it's being boiled.
'Why are you doing this to me?'
The cook knocks it down with the ladle.
'Don't try to jump out.
You think I'm torturing you,
I'm giving you flavor,
so you can mix with spices and rice
and be the lovely vitality of a human being.
Remember when you drank rain in the garden.
That was for this.'
Grace first. Sexual pleasure,

then a boiling new life begins,
and the Friend has something to eat.'[1]

The following is an ancient alchemical recipe for tincturing, that is, drawing the essence away from plants, by separating the philosopher's mercury and sulphur (which remain together in the plant kingdom) and then recombining them with the philosopher's salt to produce al-Aksir, a more potent form of herbal medicine. With some variation (for example, the mercury and the sulphur must also be separated in the mineral kingdom) this process is basically analogous to any other alchemical operation.

Combine dried or fresh chopped, ground, or powdered herb (each herb should correspond to one of the seven days of the week and one of the seven planets of antiquity and should be picked at the appropriate time of the appropriate day) with the *menstrum,* i.e, liquid extracting agent. Alcohol (al-Qohal), in the form of grain alcohol, will extract more essence from the herb than will water. (Repeated distillation of wine produces the *menstrum par excellence,* however, this process is tricky, and the results can be dangerous, and is not recommended for the novice!). Combine each herb separately with the *menstrum* in a large (quart) jar with a tight lid and shake every day. The combined ingredients should not fill over a third of the container.

Keep the jars in a warm place (but not too hot!), for example by the stove in winter, or on a sunny windowsill. Begin the operation when you see the new moon and continue the process until the full moon appears. Strain and pour off the liquid tincture into dark glass bottles (dropper bottles are best) for storage and set aside the *caput mortum* (the 'death's head' or soggy remnant of the plant), which is essential for the elixir process described below. At this point the tincture of the herb is complete and the liquid essence consists of the plant's philosophical mercury and sulphur. It may be consumed in a diluted form (a few drops in a glass of distilled water or wine) on each corresponding day of the week to bring the tonic of the body in

1. *The Mathnawi,* (III, 4160–4168), by Jalalluddin Rumi, this version: *RUMI We Are Three,* trans. by Coleman Barks (p 12)

tune with the plant and planetary forces. The psychological and intuitive learning that takes place from the actual work involved should not be underestimated!

Now, those, who chose to, will be able by *art* to take the work a next step into the most basic and primitive alchemical transformation. This process depends upon the human as intermediary between the spiritual and material planes. This next phase of the work is the formation of the herbal al-Aksir (elixir).

Saqi, dispense the water of life,
The elixir of living immortality!

'IRAQI

Al-Aksir means from or of the ashes, and the next step after the tincturing process is complete, is to take the remaining soggy herb and burn it completely to ashes. A hot fire is essential and a pyrex or other fire-resistant container (actually, few pyrex containers will withstand the temperature; a vessel made of coarse porcelain works most efficiently) in which to burn the 'death's head.' This operation should be undertaken in a well-ventilated environment that will accommodate the great amount of smoke produced. If it is done outdoors, care should be taken lest the wind blow the ashes away. A fine wire screen over the vessel will keep the ashes inside. The burning will take some time, and the burning substance will take on various characteristics and colors analogous to the classic color stages so often described in some alchemical texts. The black burning material may need to be removed from the fire and crushed repeatedly with mortar and pestle and then returned to the fire until it turns gray, and then white. This process is known as *calcination*. Next, the ashes are combined with distilled water (ideally collected thunderstorm water, distilled 7 times) and placed over a heat source. Once the water is evaporated, what remains are the hygroscopically charged *salts*.

Now the *salts*, taken from the original herb via tincturing and burning the remaining *caput mortum*, and extracted via the method described above, are recombined in a jar with some of the mercury and sulphur (the tincture) from the same plant and set in a warm, dark place for two weeks. After this incubation period the alchemically recombined plant, certainly a new thing, a Phoenix arisen from the ashes, has become a more potent medicine than the simple tincture (although mild enough, it should always be consumed in a diluted form) and is to be used exactly as it is suggested the tincture be used. This completes a most basic operation of al-Kimia.

(Adapted from Frater Albertus, Manifred M. Junius, Jean Dubuis, and Tibb Unani, with reference to Paracelsus, Albertus Magnus, and Nicholas Culpeper.)

Behold the effects of God's Mercy: How He brings the earth to life after it was dead.

QUR'AN (30:50)

APPENDIX II

THE EMERALD TABLET

ATTRIBUTED TO
HERMES TRISMEGISTOS

1. In truth, certainly and without doubt, whatever is below is like that which is above, and whatever is above is like that which is below. The highest comes from the lowest, and the lowest from the highest.
2. Just as all things proceed from One alone by meditation on One alone, so also they are born from this one thing by adaptation.
3. Its father is the sun and its mother the moon. The wind has borne it in its body. Its nurse is the earth.
4. It is the father of every miraculous work in the whole world.
5. Its power is perfect if it is converted to earth.
6. Separate the earth from the fire and the subtle from the gross, softly and with great prudence.

7. It rises from earth to heaven and comes down again from heaven to earth, and thus acquires the power of the realities above and the realities below. In this way you will acquire the glory of the whole world, and all darkness will leave you.

8. This is the power of all powers, for it conquers everything subtle and penetrates everything solid.[2]

9. Thus the little world is created according to the prototype of the great world.

10. This is the way traversed by the sages.

11. For this reason I am called Hermes Trismegistos, for I possess the three parts of wisdom of the whole world.

12. Perfect (or complete) is what I have said of the work of the sun.

2. According to Jabir Ibn Hayyan, whose original and earliest Arabic text we are here following (see: T. Burckhardt, *Alchemy*, quoting Paul Kraus, Jabir Ibn Hayyan, Cairo, 1942-43, pages 196-197), this line reveals:

When the body in its state of solidity and hardness has been so altered that it has become fine and light, it becomes as it were a spiritual thing, which penetrates bodies, although it retains its own nature, which makes it resistant to fire. At this moment it mingles with spirit, since it has become fine and loose, and its effect on the spirit is to make it constant. The fixation of the spirit in this body follows the first process, and both are transformed, each one taking on the nature of the other. The body becomes a spirit, and takes from the spirit fineness, lightness, extensibility, coloration, and all other of the spirit's properties. The spirit, for its part, becomes a body and acquires the latter's resistance to fire, immobility, and duration. From both elements a light substance is born, which possesses neither the solidity of bodies nor the fineness of spirits, but, precisely, takes up a middle position between the two extremes.

GLOSSARY

The following terms and their definitions were compiled from innumerable reading sources over a period of several years. They were originally saved in notebooks intended for personal study use only and as such were undocumented. The definitions are often brief, even fragmented, and adhere to the barest notion of 'translation' possible.

A

Abd: A male slave, the servant/creature dependent on his Lord.

Ababil: Birds.

Abduhu: 'His servant,' epithet for Muhammad (SAW) during his most sublime experience.

Abid: (pl. 'Ubbad) The devotee occupied with external acts of devotion.

Abjad: (or: Jafr) The science of numerical value configurations of the Arabic alphabet.

Adab: Spiritual refinement and good manners. The way of right action and courtesy of the Path.

Adam: Nonexistence. Innermost essence of God.

Adam Qadmon: The primordial man.

Adhan: (or: Athan or: Azan) The call to prayer.

Afrin: (pl. Afrinish) Praise and Creation.

Ahad: One.

Ahadiyya: The invisible Unity of God, known only to Himself and those who are not other than He.

Aham: (Tamil) The heart.

Ahkam: 'Orders' according to Islamic law. They are five:

    1. Compulsory (Wajib).

2. Order without obligation (Mustahab).

3. Forbidden (Moharram).

4. Disliked but not forbidden (Makruh).

5. Legal and allowed (Halal).

Ahl al-Kisa: The members of Muhammad's family who were taken under his cloak.

Ahl al-Kitab: 'People of the Book.'

Ahl as-Sunna wa'l-Jamaa: The Sunnites, the followers of the Prophetic tradition.

Ahlil Bait: The spiritual family and house of the Prophet Muhammad (SAW); all those from all times and places who have born witness to faith in the one God.

Ahwal: (pl. of Hal) Mystical States.

Ain: Seventeenth letter of the Arabic alphabet.

Ain al-Jam: 'Absolute Union' between man and God.

Akhira: (or: Akhirat) The Hereafter.

Akhlaq-i Muhammadhi: The noble qualities of the Prophet (SAW) which the believer must imitate.

Akhlat: (pl. of Khilt) Essences; humors; temperaments.

Alaihi Salam: On him be peace.

Alaikum Salam: On you be peace.

Alam al-Jabarut: The spiritual world of God and the angelic realities. Highest of the three degrees of reality.

Alam al-Malakut: The world of the soul. The psychic world between Jabarut and Mulk.

Alam al-Mithal: The world of imagination.

Alam al-Mulk: The world of physical or material existence. Lowest of the three degrees of reality.

Alastu bi Rabbikum: The Qur'anic phrase 'Am I not your Lord?'

Alhamdulillahi R-Rabbil'alameen: All praise belongs to Allah, Lord of the Worlds.

Alids: Descendants of 'Ali ibn Abi Talib.

Alif: The first letter of the Arabic alphabet, numerical value 1, cipher for God the One, the Beloved.

Alif-i Sayqal: A degree of polishing steel.

Alim: A Knower; a scholar or person of knowledge.

Alim Rabbini: A divinely inspired master.

Alin Yazisi: (Turkish) 'What is written on the forehead,' i.e., Fate.

Allah: God, the One and Only.

Allahu Akbar: God is greater.

Ama: A female slave, servant/creature dependent on her Lord. Also: Pure Being.

Amal: Action, work, or deed.

Amana: Trustworthiness.

Amanat: Something deposited into someone's trust.

Amilus salihat: Righteous deeds.

Amin: O Allah, accept our invocation. May it be so.

Ammara: The nafs in its lowest stage; blind desire and instinct; evil without conscience or self-restraint.

Amr: Divine command.

Amud: Column (of light).

An-Najwa: The private talk between Allah and each of His slaves on the Day of Resurrection.

Ana'l-Haqq: 'I am the Truth.' (Attributed to al-Hallaj).

Ana'l-Haqq Muhammadhi: The realization of true Muslimhood according to Shams-i Tabriz.

Ana Man Ahwa: 'I am he whom I love.' (al-Hallaj).

Anathi: (Tamil) The beginningless beginning prior to Athi.

Ansari: Companions of the Prophet (SAW) from Medina.

Anwar: (pl. of Nur) Lights.

Aqida: Creed, article of faith.

Aql: The mind, the intellect or pure intelligence, also: creative reason in contrast to the transcendent intellect; the same as Basirah.

Aql al-Akbar: The Greatest Intellect.

Aql al-Kull: First Intellect, or Universal Intellect.

Arba'in: Forty, as in forty-day retreat.

Arif: (pl. Arifun) The Gnostic, in contrast to the Abid and the Zahid; he who has gnosis (Ma'rifah) of God.

Arsh: The throne of God. (Persian: Dhahut).

Arwah: (pl. of Ruh) Spirits. The world of pure souls.

Ashadu an la ilaha ill'Allah: I bear witness that there is no god but God.

Ashq: (or *Ishq*) Divine love which travelers on the spiritual Path seek to find within themselves (they are called Ashiqs, Lovers) for God.

Ashraf: People who trace their lineage to the Prophet (SAW) or his companions.

Ashura: Memorial day of Husayn's martyrdom at Kerbala.

Asma: Name.

Asma al Husna: (or *Asma Ilahiyya*) The ninety-nine most beautiful names of God; the perfection of His attributes and qualities.

Asma ash Sharifa: The ninety-nine names of Muhammad (SAW).

Asr: Afternoon prayer time.

Assalalu Alaikum: Peace be upon you.

As-Suffa: The group of eighty or more Fuqara who gathered to live and learn at the Prophet's Mosque in Medina during the life of the Prophet (SAW). 'The people of the bench.'

Astaghfirullah: I ask forgiveness of God.

Athar: Trace, created thing, creature, being; in the plural it denotes multiplicity; the manifestation of the divine Qualities in the world.

Athi: (Tamil) The state of unmanifestation.

Attar: The essence of the soul of a true oil of a flower, wood, or bark.

Atiyya: Gift of Mercy.

Awliya: The saints and friends of God, plural of Wali.

Awwal: The stage at which the soul became surrounded by form and each creation took form.

Ayat: (or: Aya) Divine Sign; the verses of the Holy Qur'an.

Ayat-al-Kursi: Qu'ranic Verse #255 of Surat-al-Baqara, the Verse of the Throne.

Ayatollah: Miraculous sign of God.

Ayn: Eye.

Ayn al-Basirah: The eye of the intellect (Aql). The intellect perceives the Real but is not yet reabsorbed in it. After Shu'a al-Basirah and before Haqq al-Basirah.

Ayn al-Qalb: The eye of the heart. The intellect (Aql) as the eye of intellective vision of the Real in the heart, distinguished from the Aql as reason, situated in the brain or its subtle counterpart. The same as Basirah.

Ayn al-Yaqin: The eye of certainty. The second of three degrees of knowledge after Ilm al-Yaqin and before Haqq al-Yaqin.

Ayyar: A Rogue.

Azab: The wrath and punishment of Allah.

B

Ba: Second letter of the Arabic alphabet. The dot underneath considered by some as a symbol of 'Ali.

Baba: (Turkish) Second rank in the Bektashi Hierarchy.

Badr: Full moon.

Bahr: Ocean.

Bahrul-Ilm: The ocean of divine knowledge.

Bakht-i Siyah: Misfortune; 'Black Luck.'

Bakka'un: 'Those who constantly weep.'

Bala: Yes (as to affliction). The loving acceptance of every affliction that comes from the Beloved.

Balabailan: An artificial language used among Turkish sufis.

Banyan tree: A symbol of the Beloved.

Baqa: Subsistence, permanence; the state of reintegration in the spirit and unitive knowledge of the Absolute. The opposite of Fana (annihilation).

Baqa billah: The beginning of journeying in God after having passed through annihilation (*Fana*).

Baqara: The Cow. Title of the sacred sura of al Qur'an.

Baraka: (or *Barakat*) Blessing or divine benefit bestowed directly by God or through holy people, places, or objects.

Baraka Ya Shahim: Blessings oh my King!

Barq: Lightening.

Barrah: The pious.

Barzakh: Interval; the place between death and the awakening or resurrection.

Basair: (pl. of *Basirah*) Intuitions.

Bashir: The bringer of good tidings (al Qur'an sura 7:88).

Bashmaq-i sharif: (Turkish) The Prophet's sandal.

Basir: 'The All-Seeing,' a name of God.

Basirah: Inner vision; the intellect (Aql); the eye of the heart (Ayn al-Qalb).

Bast: Expansion in a positive spiritual sense. Opposite of Qabd (contraction).

Batin: The Inwardly Hidden; things of the unseen spiritual world.

Batiniyya: Gnostics, people of the inner meanings.

Batul: Virgin; an epithet of Fatima.

Bayat: (or: Bay'a) A pledge or promise; an oath of allegiance.

Bazgard: Restraining one's thoughts.

Be-shar: 'Without the Law;' dervishes who do not conform to the outward forms of Islamic law.

Bi-Haqq Muhammad: For Muhammad's sake. The Truth of Muhammad (SAW).

Bida: Innovation in religion.

Bidati: Heretic.

Bidhr: Seed.

Bismillah: (or: Basmala, the formula) In the name of God.

Bu: Fragrance; scent.

Bu'd: Remoteness; distance from God; opposite of Qurb (nearness to God).

Bulbul: Nightingale.

Buraq: The animal bigger than a donkey and smaller than a horse that the Prophet (SAW) rode upon during the Night of Ascension, the Miraj. An energy form of the angelic spheres.

Burda: A coat, or cloak.

Burqa: A veil.

Buruz: Exteriorization of the saint.

C

Calipha: (or *Khalifa*) The successor of the Prophet (SAW) and head of the Muslim community; in Sufism the disciple of the master authorized to transmit prayers, initiate new members, and act as the deputy or head of the Sufi order.

Char Yar: (Persian) The four friends; the first four Caliphas.

Charkinama: Religious teachings given (in poetry) in the symbolism of 'spinning.'

Chashm Rauschan: 'May your eye be bright!' Formula of congratulation.

Chilla: (or *Chillakhana*) A secluded room for spiritual practices; a forty day retreat.

Chilla-yi: Inverted Chilla: Hanging upside down for forty days.

Celebi: The title of a leader of the Bektashi order.

D

Daal: The fourth letter of the Arabic alphabet, numerical value: 4, in the fourth position of Muhammad's name.

Dahk Allah: 'God's smile' in paradise.

Dajjal: The Anti-Christ.

Dala'il: Signs.

Dargah: A spiritual shrine or meeting place for living Sufi masters. Seat of the head of an order or its branches.

Dars ul-Ambiya: The teachings of the prophets.

Darvish: (o: *Darwish, Dervish*, etc.) 'The sill of the door,' one on the threshold; a Persian name for Sufi; poor one (*Faqir*).

Daulat: The wealth of the world and/or the wealth of the grace of God.

Dawa: The summons to acknowledge religious truth.

Dayo Paree: Ghosts.

Deen: (or *Din*) Religion; the life transaction. Submission and obedience to a particular system.

Dhahut: (Persian) The throne of God (*Arsh*).

Dhat: (pl. *Dhawat*, essences) The self-subsistent essence.

Dhawq: (or *Dhauq*) Taste, intuition. 'Tasting,' immediate spiritual experience.

Dhikr: (or *Zikr; Thikr*) Remembrance, the invocation and repetition of one of the formulas or Names of God either spoken aloud, or silently, inwardly.

Dhikru'llah: The invocation/remembrance of a Name of God; fundamental to spiritual concentration in Sufism.

Dil: (Persian) Heart.

Diwan: (or *Divan*) A collection of poetry or prose.

Dua: Prayer or invocation; 'free prayer' distinguished from obligatory, ritual prayer (*Salat*).

Duha: Forenoon. Time of Ishraaq (supererogatory) prayers.

Dunya: The material world of phenomena and experience.

Durud-i sharif: (Persian) Litanies of blessings for the Prophet (SAW).

E

Efendi: (Greek) Lord.

Er: (or *Eren*, pl. *Erenler*; Turkish) True man of God.

Ezel: A place in Eternity where souls gave their response saying 'Yes' to God, that He is their Lord.

F

Fa'iq: 'The Overpowering,' a name of God.

Faid al-aqdas al-a'la: The most holy supreme flux of grace.

Fajr: Dawn or early morning before sunrise time of prayer.

Falasifa: Wise men, philosophers.

Fana: Extinction, annihilation of all that blocks the individual from God. Opposite of Baqa.

Fana Billah: Stage of annihilation when bad qualities are lost and the stage of journeying to God ends.

Fana fi Allah: Annihilation in God.

Fana fi-r-Rasul: Annihilation in the Prophet (SAW).

Fana fi'sh Shaykh: Annihilation in the spiritual guide.

Faqih: (or *Fuqaha*) A learned man who can give religious verdicts. A scholar of Fiqh.

Faqir: (pl. *Fuqura*) A poor person (usually) seeking inner wealth. Fuqura generally refers to the circle of the Prophet's companions or a Shaykh's disciples who are poor in worldly, material things but rich in the spiritual realities.

Faqirani: Feminine of *Faqir*.

Faqr: The detachment of the Spirit from all multiplicity within the mind.

Fard: (or *Farda*) Obligatory. Deed of worship.

Fardiyya: The single nature of Muhammad (SAW).

Farista: (Persian *Firishta*) Angel.

Fata: (pl. *Fityan*) The young man, the brave youth; symbol of 'Ali as mystical ideal.

Fatana: Intelligence.

Fatiha: Opening; first sura of al Qur'an, said to contain within itself the whole Qu'ran.

Fatwa: Legal decision.

Fi'l: 'Action.'

Fi sabil Allah: In the way of God, for God's sake.

Fikr: (or: Fikrah) Meditation, contemplation. Reflective thinking about the divine Attributes or Qualities.

Fiqh: Islamic law or jurisprudence.

Firdaus: The middle and the highest part of Paradise.

Fitna: The tests, trials, and difficulties of life.

Fitra: Inherent original state of the soul before it is vested in the body.

Fu'ad: Heart, as connected to Marifa.

Furjah: The human kingdom.

Furqan: Variously; a name of al Qur'an or: Islam, submission to God.

Futuh: Unsolicited gifts.

Futuwwah: Virtue. In Sufism, Futuwwah is a code of honorable conduct based on the good examples of the prophets, saints, sages, and intimate friends and lovers of God.

G

Garmi: (Persian) Warm.

Ghaflat: Heedlessness, negligence.

Ghafur: 'The Forgiver,' a name of God.

Ghani: 'The rich, Who has no need,' a name of God.

Gharaniq: Heavenly beings.

Ghauth: Help.

Ghayb: The Unseen containing the worlds of jinns, angels, disembodied souls, and other planes of existence.

Ghayba: Absence, from the world implying presence with something else.

Ghayr: (pl. *Aghyar*) The other-than-God.

Ghazal: An Arabic poetic form that passes with variations into Persian, Turkish, and Urdu poetry.

Ghazi: A fighter for the true faith.

Ghulat: Shi'a who hold 'extreme' views of the spiritual qualities of the Imam.

Ghurrul-Muhajjalun: A name given to Muslims on the Day of Resurrection referring to the glittering of the parts of their bodies that were washed in ablution.

Ghusl: A ceremonial, purifying bath in preparation for ritual prayer.

Ghwath: A Qutb that heals. A granter of requests, characterized by his vast generosity.

Gnosis: (Greek) Knowledge; to know. Wisdom of the heart.

Gnostic: Knower (Arif).

Grandshaikh: Shaikh over other Shaikhs.

Gulbang: (Turkish) A prayer of the Bektashi order.

H

Ha: A letter of the Arabic alphabet, the last letter of the name Allah, a symbol of Huwiyya.

Habib Allah: Beloved friend of God.

Habs-i Dam: Holding one's breath in recollection.

Hadi: 'The Guilding,' a name of God.

Hadir: Present.

Hadith: The Traditions of the Prophet (SAW), his sayings and deeds.

Hadith Qudsi: Sacred account; a non Qur'anic Divine Word revealed through the Prophet (SAW).

Hadiyya: Gift of Love.

Hadra: Presence; one of the modes or levels of the Divine Presence. There are five major Hadrat:

　1. *Hadrat ul-ghayb il-mutlaq*, absolute nonmanifestation, reflected in the eternal fixed essences.

　2. *Hadrat ul-ghayb il-mudaf*, relative nonmanifestation reflected in the universe of spirits.

　3. *Hadrat ul-mithal*, relative manifestation, reflected in the subtle forms.

　4. *Hadrat ul-mushahadat il-mutlaqa*, absolute manifestation reflected in the physical world.

　5. *Hadrat ul-jami'a*, the presence of the totality, reflected in the Perfect Man.

Hadrah: A gathering.

Hafira: Beginning; original state.

Hafiz: (or *Hafez*) 'The Preserver,' one of the names of God; also the title of one who memorizes al Qu'ran and preserves it in his heart.

Hahut: The Divine Essence itself. Divine ipseity.

Hajar Baht: Polished stone; Muhammad's heart.

Hajj: The pilgrimage to Mecca.

Hajji: Title of one who has performed the pilgrimage to Mecca.

Hakim: Wise.

Hal: A spiritual state; a passing state, opposed to Maqam.

Halal: Lawful, that which is permissible from the point of view of religion.

Halka: (or *Halqa*) A circle of people, usually a Shaikh and murids.

Halveti: (or *Khalwati*, secluded dervishes) One of twelve original Tariqats which follow a line of transmission through Shaikh Omar al Khalwati.

Hama ust: (Persian) 'Everything is He.'

Hamd: Praise, due to God; the root of the names Muhammad and Ahmad.

Hamdu lillahi: Praise be to God!

Hamida: To laud, to praise.

Hanif: Worshiping God alone, associating no thing or person with Him.

Haqiqat: (or *Haqiqah*) Inner Reality. In Sufism, the stage beyond Tariqat where the seeker sees things as they truly exist. Esoteric truth, the Divine Reality.

Haqiqat Muhammadiyya: The Reality of Muhammad (SAW), the archetypal prophet.

Haqq: Ultimate Truth, a name or attribute of God.

Haqq al-Basirah: The Truth of the intellect; the third and final perception of the Real after Shu'a al-Basirah and Ayn al-Basirah; corresponds to Haqq al-Yaqin; where all duality disappears.

Haqq al-Yaqin: The truth of certitude; the third and final degree of certitude with regard to the Absolute; corresponds to Haqq al-Basirah; comes after Ayn al-Yaqin.

Haram: Unlawful, forbidden and punishable from the point of view of religion.

Hasbi Allah: God is sufficient.

Hashr: Gathering. The title of sura fifty-nine of al Qur'an.

Haya: Modesty, self-respect, scruples. Haya can be good or bad, the good Haya is to be ashamed to do that which God has forbidden, or to not do a thing that God has ordered.

Hayaman: Bewilderment and Passion.

Hayat: The Ruh (soul) of the plenitude and completeness of man's life.

Hayba: Reverence and awe before God's majesty.

Hayy: The Ever-Living. One of the ninety-nine names of God.

Hazir u Nazir: Present and watching; referring to the Holy Prophet (SAW).

Hazirat al-quds: The Sphere of Holiness.

Hazreti: (or *Hazrat, Hadrat*) 'Noble presence,' a title of respect given to saints.

Hegira: (or *Hijra*, etc.) The emigration of the Prophet Muhammad (SAW) from Mecca to Medina (A.D. 622), when the Muslims calendar begins.

Hijab al-Azamah: The 'Veil of Majesty' before God.

Hijab al-Marifa: The 'Veil of Gnosis.'

Hikam: (or *Hikamat*) Wisdom.

Hikmat-i Yamani: Intuitive wisdom.

Hikmat-i Yunani: 'Greek' wisdom.

Hilm: Forbearance, moderation, tranquility in the face of passion.

Hilya: 'Ornament.' Description of Muhammad's qualities.

Himma: Spiritual yearning, drive, or ambition.

Hirs: Greed.

Hizb: Litany; a special prayer formula.

Hizmet: (or *Khidhmat*) Service. In Sufism, any service is done only for God's sake.

Houris: Very fair females created by God and not the offspring of Adam with intense dark eyes.

Hubb: A name for Love.

Hubb 'urdhri: Platonic love.

Hubut: The Fall of mankind from the Garden of Eden.

Hudur wa ghayba: Presence near God and absence from oneself.

Hujja: Proof; the person through whom God's presence becomes accessible.

Hujrah: A shaykh's meditation cell.

Hulul: Indwelling; as in incarnation.

Hush dar dam: Awareness in breathing.

Husn az-zann: To think well of God.

Husn u Ishq: Beauty and Love.

Husna: The Beauty; the beauty that is the inner form of man.

Huwa: He.

Huwa Huwa: Exactly He. God created Adam as 'exactly he.'

Huwiyya: From the pronoun *Huwa*, 'He': the ineffable Divine Identity; God Himself transcending attribute or description.

I

Ibadat: (or *Ibada*) Spiritual service or worship including prayer, work, and Dhikr.

Ibn al-Waqt: The Son of the Moment; he who lives in the present, not in the past or future.

Id: (o: *Eid*, *Eed*, etc.) The Muslim festivals.

Idhn: Permission, authority to guide others on the Path.

Ifshar as-Sirr: Divulgence of the secret.

Iftar: The food eaten to end a fast.

Ihsan: The highest level of deeds and worship. Virtue.

I'jaz: Inimitability of al-Qur'an.

Ilahi: A song praising God.

Ilm: Knowledge or science.

Ilm Ladunni: Divinely inspired knowledge.

Ilm al-Yaqin: Knowledge or certitude.

Iltibas: Concealment of pre-eternal beauty.

Imam: The person who leads Islamic prayers, or the Muslim Caliph.

Iman: True faith. In Sufism, this is the second of the three stations of Islam, not first as in exoteric Islam: Islam, Imam, Ihsan.

Inaba: Return from minor sins to Love.

Insan: The true form of the human being.

Insan Kamil: A complete, perfected, God realized being.

Insha'Allah: If God wills.

Intiqal-i Nisbat: Transferal of spiritual qualities.

Iqama: The statements of the Adhan recited once before obligatory prayers are offered.

Iqamat as-Salat: The offering of the obligatory prayers perfectly just as the Prophet (SAW) performed them.

Iqan: Assurance.

Irfan: Gnosis, knowledge.

Irshad: Guidance, direction; instruction for inner growth.

Isha: Night prayer beginning an hour and a half after sunset (approximately). The fifth prayer time.

Isharat: Mystical hints, allusions.

Ishq: (see *Ashq*) Passionate love for God.

Ishq–i Haqiqi: Love of Truth; love of God.

Ishq-i Majazi: Love for created things.

Ishtiqaq Kabir: Gematria; the derivation of separate words from each letter of a word.

Islam: Complete surrender and submission to God.

Ism-i Azam: The Greatest Name of God. (Unknown?).

Isma: The infallibility of the Prophet (SAW), who is protected from sins.

Isnad: Chain of transmission.

Isra: The night journey.

Istidlali: Insight gained through inference.

Istighfar: Seeking God's forgiveness.

Istihlak: Absorption.

Istiskhara: A specific prayer for guidance concerning a certain matter.

I'tikaf: Seclusion in a mosque for the purpose of worshiping Allah only.

Ithar: To prefer others to oneself.

Ithbat: The affirmation of what God has ordained.

Itminan: Tranquility.

Ittihad: Union of lover with the Beloved.

J

Jabarut: The sphere of divine knowledge or Ilm; the sphere of God's power.

Jabr: Predestination.

Jadhba: Celestial Attraction in the form of grace and blessings exerted upon those following the Path, especially on the Majdoub.

Jadhbi: Reached by Jadhba.

Jafr: Exegetical analysis of the letters of al Qur'an.

Jahannum: Hell.

Jalal: Divine Majesty.

Jalis Allah: 'Who sits with God.'

Jam al-Jam: 'Perfect collectedness;' the last stage of union.

Jam'u Tafriqa: Collectedness and separation.

Jamal: Divine Beauty.

Jamat: (or: Jama'a) The community collective; associated with Jumah, the Friday congregational prayers.

Jami: 'The Comprising;'; a name of God.

Jami': The largest community mosque.

Jannat: Garden. Usually refers to Paradise.

Jasim: Noble.

Jasimun: 'Great in dignity.'

Jawanmard: Virtuous young man.

Jihad: Holy fighting in the cause of Allah.

Jihad al Akbar: The greatest fight or struggle. The Prophet Muhammad (SAW) said that the greatest struggle is Jihad an-Nafs, the struggle with the self; the desires and ego of the seeker.

Jinn: A Creation of God's made from fire; like human beings from mud, angels from light.

Ju al-Baqar: Voracity; infinite hunger for love.

Jumah: Friday. The first day of the Muslim Week and also the name of the Friday community prayer service.

Juz: One-thirtieth of al Qur'an.

K

Kaaba: (or: Ka'bah, etc.) The cube-shaped original House of the one God built by Adam, later rebuilt by Abraham and Muhammad (SAW), containing the Black Stone. Its location in Mecca determines the direction Muslims pray and worship.

Kabir: Great, large.

Kalam: Theology.

Kalb: A Dog: That which lies in front of the station of the Qalb is the dog of desire.

Kalima: The Islamic creed: There is no god but God, Muhammad is His Prophet and Messenger.

Kamal: Divine perfection.

Karabkht: Black luck; misfortune.

Karamah: (or: Karamat) A 'miracle' instigated by a Saint.

Karim: 'The Generous;' a name of God.

Kashf: Unveiling; revelation.

Kashf 'Aqli: Revelation of the plane of reason.

Kashf Ilahi: Revelation in the heart.

Kashf Imani: Revelation through faith.

Kashf Kauni: Revelation through created things.

Kathafat: Gross matter which is however needed to reveal the spiritual.

Kauthar: A sacred river or fountain in Paradise.

Khafi: Innermost secret.

Khair: That which is acceptable to wisdom and to Allah.

Khaleel: (or: Khalil, etc.) More than a friend or beloved, i.e., one who's love is mixed with one's soul. Allah is Muhammad's Khaleel.

Khalifa: Caliph.

Khalilullah: Title of Prophet Abraham meaning Friend of God.

Khaliq Jabbar: The Overpowering Creator.

Khalq: The Creation, or entire Universe distinguished from al-Haqq, the Truth, or uncreated Real, the ontological Principle of Creation.

Khalwat: Retreat for prayer and seclusion.

Khalwat dar Anjuman: Solitude in the crowd.

Khamush: Silent!

Khamyaza: 'Yawning;' the insatiable longing of man for God.

Khaniqah: (or: Khanqa, etc.) A retreat house and gathering place for dervishes.

Kharabat: 'Taverns'; 'ruins'; where treasure if found.

Khariq ul-Ada: What breaks the custom, the norm; miracles.

Khatam al-Anbiya: Seal of the prophets.

Khatam al-Auliya: Seal of the saints.

Khatir: (pl. Khawatir) Ideas that suddenly come into one's heart.

Khatm al-Wilaya: Seal of saintship.

Khawf: Fear of God.

Khidiw: Sovereign.

Khirqa: The patched cloak passed from the Sufi master to the initiate as a symbol of the communication of the blessings inherited from the Prophet (SAW).

Khirqa-i Sharif: The Prophet's cloak.

Khirqa-yi Irada: From the educating master.

Khirqa-yi Tabarruk: For the sake of blessing.

Khulafa ar-Rashidun: The 'rightly guided caliphs,' the first four successors of Muhammad (SAW).

Khumra: A small mat just sufficient for the hands and face (prostrating during prayers).

Khutba: Sermon.

Kibrit Ahmar: Red sulphur; symbol of the alchemistic activity of the shaykh.

Kiswa: The black and gold-embroidered veil for the Kaaba.

Koran: (See: Qu'ran).

Kufr: *Kufr* means: to cover up reality. A Kafir is one who does so.

Kufr-i Tariqat: Infidelity on the Path; state of intoxication.

Kulah: A type of hat worn by Shaykhs or dervishes.

Kull: Universal.

Kun: Be. The word of God with which He caused everything to Be.

Kun fa-Yakun: 'Be, and it becomes;' God's creative word.

Kusuf: Solar eclipse.

L

La: No. Particle of negation.

La ana illa ana: There is no I but I.

La Hawla Kuwata illa bila: There is no strength and no power except with God.

La Ilaha Ila'lla: 'There is no god but God.' The first section of the Kalima.

La ilaha illa'Ishq: There is no god but Love.

La Maujuda illa Allah: There is nothing existing except God.

Labaik: I respond to Your call, I am obedient to Your orders.

Lahut: Divine nature revealing itself.

Lailat al-Qadr: The Night of Might, or of Power in which al-Qur'an was first revealed.

Lam: The arabic letter which represents an-Nur to the transformed person.

Latafat: Fineness. The spiritual side of things.

Lataif: Touches of grace; subtle centers in the body.

Latif: 'The Subtle'; a name of God.

Lauha: (Turkish: Levha) Tablet.

Lawa'ih: Outward appearance, looks, signs. A temporary, or passing state of enlightenment.

Lawa'ih Lawhiyya: Surface signs, or outward appearances of the tablet.

Lawamma: Conscience; the ability to see and accuse the Nafs of wrongdoing.

Lawh al-Mafuz: The Guarded Tablet in which all destinies are written, identical with the Throne of Mercy (Sarir al-Rahmaniyya).

Lisan ul-Hal: Silent eloquence; speaking though one's whole being.

Liwa al-Hamd: The flag of praise, which Muhammad (SAW) carries.

Lubb: Innermost heart.

Lutf: Divine kindness.

M

Ma sha Allah: May it please God, or: As it pleases God.

Ma'shuq: The Beloved.

Ma'siya: Rebellion, sin.

Ma'sum: A person who possesses 'Isma, infallibility, freedom from committing sins.

Maddahun ar-Rasul: Those who professionally recite praise songs for the Prophet (SAW).

Madhhab: A religious school.

Maghazi: The Prophet's wars and the literature connected with them.

Maghrib: West, indicates time of sunset and obligatory prayer.

Mahabba: Love.

Mahal: House or level.

Mahbubiyyat-i Khuda: Muhammad's rank as God's beloved friend.

Mahdi: 'Who is guided' and appears at the end of time to fill the world with justice.

Mahfil: Gathering.

Mahmud: Praiseworthy.

Mahq: Obliteration; the unchanging state of not being able to see even one's self. It is the state above Mahw in which traces of the self remain. Jili states that Mahq is the state of the vice-regency of God and its perfection does not belong to this world.

Mahq al-Mahq: Obliteration of obliteration; the concealment of the vice-regency destined by God to the true human being. Jili states that Mahq al-Mahq may be perfected in this world.

Mahsus: Special, particular, reserved for.

Mahw: The elimination of one's habits; the erasure of errors from the visible self, of unconsciousness from the heart, and of the tendency to see other than God from the soul.

Majd: Glory.

Majdhoub: One experiencing divine intoxication; 'Mad-in-the-Divine.'

Makr: Plot; ruse.

Maktub: Fate; that which is written.

Mala al-Ala: The Supreme Company, the Angels.

Mala'ikah: (singular: Malak) Angels.

Malakut: The hidden world.

Malamiyya: (or: *Malamatiyya*, Melamiyyat) Those Sufis whose discipline is to take blame upon themselves, accepting the world's attribution of guilt while remaining secretly innocent. Ibn Arabi applies this term to the highest grade of Sufis, who embody the secret of Muhammad (SAW).

Malang: Itinerant dervish.

Malfuzat: Sayings of the Sufi Masters.

Maqam: A stage or level of spiritual development. A stopping or resting place, a station.

Maqam al-Mahmud: The highest place in paradise granted to Muhammad (SAW) exclusively.

Marbub: 'Who has a lord;' a named thing ruled by the Name in Ibn Arabi's system.

Mard: Man.

Mard-i Momin: 'The believer,' in Iqbal's terminology the truly perfected Muslim.

Mardudun: (singular: *Mardud*) Those sent back; Ibn Arabi's term for those who, having attained the Presence of God, are returned by Him to His creation.

Marifat: (or *Ma'rifah*) Stage of knowledge and realization which follows Haqiqat. Gnosis.

Marwa: A mountain in Mecca neighboring the Great Mosque.

Masih: Messiah; Christ.

Masjid: Mosque.

Masjid al-Aqsa: The great mosque in Jerusalem.

Masjid al-Haram: The great mosque in Mecca where the Kaaba is located.

Matem: Mourning.

Mathnawi: A poem in rhyming distichs (couplets) common in Persian, Turkish, and Urdu.

Maulid: Birth.

Maut: (or: Mawt) Death.

Mawadda: Love, charity.

Mawaliya: Short Arabic popular poem

Mawatin: (singular: *Mawtin*) Realms; Ibn Arabi's term for the ultimate grounds or 'homelands' of all created experience. They are: pre-Creation, this world, the subtle world, Resurrection, Hell/Paradise, and the site of the Divine Vision 'outside of Paradise.'

Mawlana: Our Master or our helper. Title of honor.

Maya: Illusion; al-Dunya.

Mecca: The Arabian capital and most sacred of the Islamic world; it is the birthplace of the Prophet Muhammad (SAW) and the site of the Kaaba.

Medina al-Munawwara: The Illuminated City, burial place of the Prophet Muhammad (SAW).

Merhaba: Welcome.

mhmd: The consonants of Muhammad's name.

Mihr: (Persian) Kindness; sun.

Mihrab: An alcove or prayer niche which indicates the direction of prayer.

Milad: Birthday.

Mim Dausi: Prayer connected with the Arabic letter M or 'meem' in the Turkish Bektashi order.

Minaret: The tower of a mosque from which the call to prayer is called.

Minbar: The high seat or chair in a mosque from which the Khutba is delivered.

Minnat: Gratitude as a burden and obligation.

Mirad: An arrow without a head.

Miraj: Ladder, or: Ascent. Refers to the 'night journey' of Muhammad (SAW) known as *Isra*.

Misbah: Lamp.

Mithal: Image or symbol.

Mithaq: Covenant.

Mohkam: Qur'anic suras which are not abrogated.

Molla Hunkar: Head of the Mevlevis.

Mu'adhdhin: (or *Muezzin*, etc.) The one who makes the call to prayer.

Mu'amalat: Muslim laws pertaining to social relations.

Mu'ataba: Blaming.

Mu'jizah: (or *Mu'jizo*) A divine miracle, an act beyond natural laws and reasoning.

Mu'min: A true believer, one with true Iman.

Mu'wwidhat: Surat al-Falaq (113) and Surat an-Nas (114); last two suras of al-Qur'anic together.

Mubarakat: The supreme, imperishable treasure of all three worlds; the beginning (Awwal), this world (Dunya), and the hereafter (Akhir). The blessings of God.

Mubashshirat: Glad tidings.

Mubiqat: (or *al-Kaba'ir*) Great destructive sins.

Mudhammam: Blameworthy.

Mudill: 'Who leads astray,' a name of God.

Mufarrih: Tranquilizer.

Mufti: A lawyer who gives a legal decision.

Muhabbat: Discourse or teaching.

Muhammad Rasul Allah: 'Muhammad is God's messenger,' the second part of the *Kalimah*.

Muhasaba: Analysis of the soul.

Muhibb: Lover.

Muhit: 'The All-Encompassing,' a name of God manifested in His throne.

Muhyi: 'He who gives life,' a name of God.

Mujaddid: 'The renewer,' the scholar or holy-man who comes once every century to restore the true knowledge and practice of Islam.

Mujahid: A warrior in God's army for the purity of Islam.

Mujazziz: (or *Qa'if*) A learned person who reads the foot and hand marks.

Mujtahadin: Independent religious scholars who do not follow religious opinions based on other than al-Qur'an and the Prophet's Sunna.

Mukhaddarat-i Abdaliyya: A group of women saints in Sind.

Mukhlas: 'Who has been made sincere.'

Mukhlis: 'Who practices sincerity.'

Mulhidun: Heretical.

Mullah: A learned man, equivalent of 'Alim.

Mulk Lak: 'Thine is the kingdom,' Dhikr of the stork.

Mumit: 'He who gives death,' a name of God.

Munajat: Intimate conversation; prayer, orison.

Munaqara: Contest of saints.

Muqaddim: 'One who brings forward.' A Sheikh's assistant or second.

Muqtasid: A moderate, who loves God for Himself.

Muraqaba: Contemplation.

Murid: One with desire; a novice on the spiritual path, one who has abandoned his will to the teacher in order to discover who he is.

Murshid: Teacher; guide, a Sufi shaykh.

Muruwwat: Virtue.

Musafir: A traveler.

Musalla: A praying carpet or place.

Mushaf: Copy of al-Qur'an.

Mushahada: Contemplation, vision.

Muslim: One who accepts submission to God and follows the way of life of Islam, a believer in God.

Mustahlikun: (singular: *Mustahlik*) Ibn Arabi's expression for those lost in the contemplation of God's Unity to the exclusion of His manifestation in multiplicity. Not as high as Mardudun, also see: *Istihlak*.

Mustajab as-Dua: One whose prayers are answered.

Mustawif: Pretender to Sufism.

Muta: He who is obeyed.

Mutafahish: One who conveys evil talk.

Mutajarrid: The recluse, the contemplative who withdraws from society and leads the life of mendicancy. He lives in a state of Tajrid.

Mutakif: A person in seclusion during Itikaf.

Mutasabbib: A sufi who lives in the midst of society and earns his own living.

Mutasabbir: He who attempts to be patient.

Mutasawwif: One who aspires to become a Sufi.

Mutashabihat: Qur'anic suras which are hard to understand.

Mutawakkil: A person who has reached Tawakkal, unwavering trust in God.

Muti: He who obeys.

Mutmainnah: When the Nafs is at rest and not a victim to itself.

Mutras: (Persian) 'Don't be afraid.'

Muwahhid: Confessor of Unity.

Muwashshah: Popular Arabic strophic poem.

Muzdawij: Arabic poems with rhyming couplets.

Myein: (Greek) To close the eyes.

N

Na'am: Yes.

Na't: (or *Natiyya*) Poetry in praise of the Prophet (SAW).

Nabi: (pl. *Anbiya*) Prophet.

Nabi Mustapha Rasool: Nabi, Prophet, Mustapha, the chosen one, Rasul, the messenger. A name used for Prophet Muhammad (SAW).

Nadhir: Warner.

Nafas: The breath of the spirit; pulse.

Nafas ar-Rahman: The Breath of the Merciful.

Nafs: Self, desires, ego. There is no veil between God and His servant except the Nafs.

Nafs al-Ammara: The 'soul that inspires evil.'

Nafs al-Lawwama: The 'blaming soul.'

Nafs al-Mutma'inna: The 'soul at peace.'

Nafs al-Qaddisa: The 'sanctified soul.'

Nafsi Nafsi: 'I myself.' Exclamation of the prophets on Judgement Day.

Najat: Help.

Najwa: Confidential talk between God and His devotees on the Day of Judgment.

Nam: (Persian) Dew.

Namaz: (Persian, Urdu, Turkish) Prayer, worship, Salat.

Namus: 'Nomos,' an angelic figure.

Naqshbandi: (or *Naqshbandiyya*) One of the official Tariqat orders with lines of transmission through Pir Muhammad Naqshbandi.

Nardaban: (Persian) Ladder.

Nasim: Graceful.

Nasimun: Gentle.

Naskh: Abolition; also: cursive script.

Nasut: Human nature in God.

Nawfil: (or *Nawafil*, Nafila, etc.) Optional practice of worship in contrast to obligatory (*Farda*).

Naz: Coquettery; a quality of the beloved.

Nazar: Vision, or 'looking.'

Nazar bar Qadam: Watching over one's steps.

Nefes: A Turkish religious song.

Ni'ma: Bounty.

Nigah Dasht: To watch one's thoughts.

Nikah: Marriage according to Islamic law.

Niyaz: Supplication or offerings in the name of Allah or His Prophet (SAW). Refers to the dervish bow or salute to the divine possibility in the other.

Niyyah: (or *Niyyat*) Intention; formal declaration to do something.

Nubuwwa: Prophethood.

Nun: Fish.

Nuni: The name of an angel, as corresponds to the shape of the arabic letter 'N' or nuun, the personification of the First Intellect in its passive aspect as the container of all knowledges.

Nur: (pl. *Anwar*) Light, brilliance, spiritual luminescence; a name of God. The Light of Allah.

Nur Muhammad: The beauty of the qualities and actions of the Wilayats (powers) of God. That beauty is the beauty of the face or countenance. 'The Light of Muhammad.' 'Muhammad's existent Light.'

Nusk: Religious acts of worship.

Nusuk: A sacrifice.

P

Paighambar Gul: The Prophet's flower, as part of his spirit.

Partiya: (Tamil) 'Have you seen?'

Parwana: Moth.

Pir: An elder. A shaykh or murshid of a high order, often the founder of an order through which lines of Tariqat pass.

Post: Sitting place for a shaykh.

Postnishin: Successor.

Prema: Unfulfilled love.

Purbi: 'Eastern' language.

Purusa Sakta: 'Primordial man' in the Hindu tradition.

Q

Qa'im al-Layl wa Sa'im ad-Dahr: 'Who stays awake during the night and fasts constantly.'

Qaba Qausain: 'Two bows length' distance of Muhammad from God (see Sura 53:9 in al-Qur'an).

Qabd: Contraction, closing. Diminution of self by withdrawing from the surface personality toward the interior.

Qadam Rasul: The Prophet's footprints in stone.

Qadar: Free will; or: predestination.

Qadi: A judge.

Qaf-i Qurb: The limit of proximity.

Qahr: Divine Wrath.

Qalabiyya: Outward form.

Qalam, al: The Pen, title of the Seventieth Sura. Used by Ibn Arabi as a parallel philosophical term for the First Intellect.

Qalandar: Member of a wandering dervish order who cares not for outward forms.

Qalb: Heart; mind; soul; choicest part; genuine, pure. The heart within the heart; the inner heart.

Qana'at: Contentment.

Qari: (pl. *Qurra*) One well versed in knowledge of al-Qur'an. (See also: *Hafiz*).

Qasida: Poem, chanted song, or mystic story told in verse.

Qasim: 'Well shaped.'

Qasimun: Handsome. Surname of the Prophet (SAW).

Qaul: Word.

Qawm: Lineage; tribe; religious community; nation.

Qawwali: Religious folk songs preformed by groups of singers from the Qawwal (mainly Indo-Pakistan).

Qayyum: The highest saint, through which the world persists according to Sirhindi's theology. (See also: Qutb). A later Indian Naqshbandi theory.

Qibla: The direction of the Kaaba in Mecca and the direction toward which Muslims face to pray. Also refers to the Throne of God within the heart.

Qidam: God's pre-eternity.

Qil (and *Qal*): Idle talk.

Qillat al-Kalam: 'Little speech.'

Qillat al-Manam: 'Little sleep.'

Qillat at-Ta'am: 'Little food.'

Qiyam: The posture of standing in prayer.

Qiyyamat: The Day of Resurrection. See also: Yawm al-Qiyamah.

Qubba: Small sanctuary.

Qudrat: Power, strength. Refers also to moments of power that if not seized are lost.

Qul: 'Say!' Divine address in al-Qur'an.

Qum: 'Rise!' (See Sura 74:1 in al-Qur'an).

Qunut: Invocation in the prayer.

Qu'ran: Recitation. The revealed scripture of Islamic faith, conveyed by the angel Gabriel (*Jabril*) to the Prophet Muhammad (SAW) over a period of twenty three years. It contains 6,666 verses or 114 chapters (*Suras*).

Qurb: Nearness; proximity; approach; neighborhood.

Qurb al-Fara'id: Nearness to God by means of the legally prescribed duties.

Qurb an-Nawafil: Nearness to God by means of superogatory works of piety.

Qurban: An animal sacrificed to God and then distributed charitably.

Qussas: (sing: *qass*) Popular preachers.

Qutb: Axis or pole, pivot of the universe; the highest station in the Sufi hierarchy of saints. The Qutb is said to be the successor of Muhammad (SAW) and is responsible for the welfare of the entire world. Only truly understood by the person who has attained it.

Qutbiyat: The wisdom which is the Wilayat of the Qutb.

Quwwat-i Qudsiyya: Faculty of sanctity.

R

Ra'is: Person of high rank, a headman or chief.

Ra'uf: 'Mild,' name of God and of the Prophet.

Rabb: Lord, owner. Designation or name of God.

Rabita Kurmak: 'Establish a tie,' between master and disciple.

Radiy Allahu 'anhu: (abbreviated: r.a.a.) 'May God be pleased with him.'

Refraf: Mysterious heavenly vehicle or cushion (see: Sura 55:76 in al-Qur'an).

Rahma: Mercy.

Rahman: Merciful. A name of God. The compassion which fills the whole universe.

Rahmatan lil-Alamin: 'Mercy for the worlds.'

Rahmatu Llah Alayhi: (abbreviated: r.a.) 'May the blessings of God be upon him.'

Rahmatul-al ameen: The mercy and compassion of the One who gives everything to all His creations.

Raiyan: The gates of Paradise through which the people who often fast will enter.

Raja: Hope.

Rajul: Man of God; The Gnostic.

Rak'a: (pl. *Rak'at*) The Muslim ritual prayer consists of different numbers of *Rak'a*, which means one bowing and two prostrations.

Ramadan: The month of ritual fasting in Islam, the month when the Holy Qur'an began to be revealed.

Raqib: 'The watcher' in Arabic love poetry.

Rashidun: The rightly guided, a title applied to the first four Caliphs.

Rasul Allah: The Messenger of God (SAW); the Prophet Muhammad (SAW).

Rasulun Karim: 'The noble Messenger.' Surname of Muhammad (SAW).

Raziq: 'The Nourisher,' a name of God.

Razzaq: 'He who bestows Rizq,' a name of God.

Rehber: The guide.

Riba: Usury.

Ribat: Convent.

Rida: Contentment.

Rind: 'Drunkard,' spiritually free, ecstatic person.

Risala: Office of the Rasul.

Riya: Hypocrisy.

Riyada: Training of character through ascetic practices.

Rizq: Nourishment; food; sustenance; livelihood. 'Daily bread.'

Rouh-ul-Lah: The Breath, the Soul, the Word of God; Jesus.

Ruba'i: Quatrain.

Rububiyya: Divine Lordship.

Ruh: The soul; essence; breath of God; revelation.

Ruhi: Spiritual principle.

Ruhul Quddus: The Holy Spirit.

Rukh: Cheek.

Rukhsa: (pl. *Rukhas*) Indulgence.

S

Saad: Arabic letter; symbolizes the eye.

Sab'a al-Mathani: The seven most recited Ayat (verses) of al-Qur'an: Surat al-Fatiha.

Sabab: (pl. *Asbab*) Cause, secondary cause, means of livelihood, profession, trade.

Sabik: 'The preceding,' who has annihilated his will in God's will.

Sabir: Patient.

Sabur: (o: *Sabr, Saboor*) 'The Patient.' One of the names of God.

Sabzpush: 'Wearing green,' the highest saints, prophets, and angels.

Sadaqa: Anything given in charity seeking only God's pleasure.

Sadr: Breast.

Safa: Purity.

Safar Dar Watan: Internal journey according to the Naqshbandi theories.

Saff: A line or row, usually refers to prayer or battle. Rank.

Safi: Pure.

Sah'ra: Desert.

Sahaba: The companions of the Prophet (SAW).

Sahib: Rightful owner or master.

Sahu: Forgetting.

Sahw: Sobriety.

Sair Ila al-Ashya: 'Traveling towards the things,' the return of the mystic from the Divine Present into daily life.

Saiyid: Master. Also used as a title for the descendants of Muhammad (SAW).

Saiyidi: 'My master.'

Sajada: When certain Ayat of certain Suras of al-Qur'an are read, it becomes essential to make a prostration.

Sajdah: The posture of prostration in Islamic prayer.

Sajjada: Prayer rug.

Saki: (or *Saqi*) The wine bearer or pourer of the saki, the drink of divine ecstasy.

Sakina: Tranquility, calmness. Divine presence.

Salaams: The greeting of peace.

Salat: The five-times-per-day obligatory Islamic prayer.

Salat Maqluba: Performing the prayer hanging upside-down.

Salawat: The wishing of prayers and blessings of God upon The Prophet Muhammad.

Salawat al-Mashishiyya: Formulas of blessing upon the Prophet (SAW) attributed to Ibn Mashish.

Salawat Tabriqieh: A special Salawat used in certain Sufi gatherings.

Salih: (pl. *Salihun*) A developed man; one who is in the right place at the right time.

Salik: Wayfarer on the path.

Sallallahu 'Alahi Wasallam: 'May the peace and blessings of God be upon him.' A supplication mentioned after the name of the Prophet Muhammad (SAW).

Sama: Heaven; also: ecstatic contemplation, audition. Mystical dance.

Sama Khana: A room for Sama.

Samad: 'Eternal,' one of the names of God.

Samadiyyat: State of eternity.

Sanam: Idol.

Sanjak: Flag or standard.

Sardi: (Persian) Cold.

Sarir al-Rahmaniyya: The Throne of Mercy, called also the Guarded Tablet, is the Soul of the Universe. Every destiny and every knowledge are encompassed by it.

Sarniwisht: 'What is written on the head.' Fate.

Sarwar-i Kan'inat: 'The leader of the Universe.'

Satpanth: The 'true path.'

Sattar: 'The Veiler' (who covers human sins), a name of God.

Saum: Fasting, or the Fast.

Sauma'a: Monastery.

Saum da'udi: Fasting one day, eating one day.

(SAW): Common abbreviation for Sallallahu 'Alahi Wasallam

Shab-i Barat: Full moon in the month of Shaban, in which the destinies of the coming year are fixed.

Shafa'a: Muhammad's intercession.

Shafi: Intercessor.

Shah: (Persian) King.

Shahada: The process of bearing testimony to the Kalima and declaring oneself a Muslim. The profession of faith.

Shaheed: (or *Shahid*) A martyr. One who witnesses for God by the sacrifice of their life. A witness.

Shahwa: Craving, natural appetite.

Shaitan: The Devil. The chief of evil ones. Symbol of Nafs.

Shajarah: The listing of names of Shaykhs of a *Silsilah*.

Shakur: 'The Thankful,' a name of God.

Sham-i Mahfil: 'The candle of the assembly,' the most radiant and attractive person in a gathering.

Shama'il: Good qualities.

Shams: Sun.

Shaqq al-Qamar: 'Splitting of the moon.'

Shariat: (or *Shariah*) The divine laws and codes for human life, conveyed by all prophets; corrected, completed and sealed in the Holy Qur'an.

Sharif: A descendant of the Prophet Muhammad (SAW).

Sharq: The East, home of illumination.

Sharr: That which is wrong, bad, or evil; as opposed to Khair (right).

Shasuwar: Princely rider.

Shathliyat: 'Theopathic locutions' paradoxes of the Sufis.

Shaykh: (or: *Sheikh*, etc.) 'old man,' a master, spiritual guide; title of a teacher of Sufism.

Shaykha: Female *shaykh* or spiritual leader.

Sherif: One's place; also the sitting place of the Shaikh or representatives of the Prophet (SAW).

Shi'a: The group of Muslims who regard 'Ali and his heirs as the only legitimate successors to the Prophet, divided into sects according to allegiance to different lines of 'Alid descent.

Shi'at 'Ali: The party of 'Ali.

Shifa: Healing. Also the title of Avicenna's medical encyclopedia.

Shirk: To worship other than God. Polytheism.

Shirk Khafi: Hidden associationism.

Shu'a' al-Basirah: The ray of light of the intellect.

Siddiq: A person who is true.

Sidi: 'My Lord,' appellation of Muhammad (SAW).

Sidr: Lotus tree.

Sidrah: High council of Shaykhs.

Sidrat-ul-Muntaha: A tree over the seventh heaven, the Lote tree of the farthest regions in spheres near to the divine presence.

Sifat: The manifestation of creation; attributes; all that has come into appearance as form; that which arose from the word 'Kun! (Be!).'

Siharfi: Golden alphabet.

Sihr Halal: 'Licit magic' = poetry.

Sikke: A type of tall dervish hat of the Mevlevi order.

Silsilah: Line of transmission from master to master of the spiritual power and teaching of a Tariqat.

Simurgh: Mythical bird. See: Attar's 'Conference of the Birds.'

Sirajun Munir: 'A radiant lamp,' surname of the Prophet (SAW) see Sura 33:45 in al-Qur'an.

Sirat al-Mustaqim: The straight path; the path of right guidance ordained by the Holy Qur'an.

Sirr: Divine secrets; the greatest mystery; root; origin.

Sirr al-Khususiyyah: The particular charismatic attributes of a seeker in the Path.

Sirr-i Dilbaran: The secret of the beloved ones.

Siyam: A fast (particularly during Ramadan).

Sofra: The tablecloth spread for eating.

Sophos: Wise.

Stirb und Werde: (German) Die and become.

Subhan-Allah: Glory be to God!

Subhana Rabbi al'Ala: Glory to God Most High!

Subhani: 'Glory be to me!' Bayazid's Shath.

Suf: Wool.

Sufi: A Muslim mystic. (For Sufism, see: Tasawwuf).

Suhbat: (also *Sohbet*) Spiritual conversation between master and disciple.

Suhur: A meal taken before the Fajr prayer on the nights of fasting during Ramadan.

Sukr: Intoxication.

Suluk: Wandering on the path (see Salik).

Sunna: All the traditions and practices of the Prophet Muhammad (SAW) that have become models to be followed by Muslims.

Sunnis: The majority of the Muslim community who accept the Sunna and the historical succession of Caliphs as opposed to the 'Alids (Shi'a).

Sunnitrash: 'Sunnicizer,' a strict adherent to the Sunna.

Sura: (pl. *Surat*) Form, whether physical, subtle, or abstract. Term refers to a chapter of al-Qur'an.

Suratul-Fatihah: The opening chapter of al-Qur'an that must be recited at the beginning of every ritual Islamic prayer.

Suryani: Mystical language.

T

Ta'ifa: A group, a branch, or a guild.

Ta'widh: A written or spoken religious amulet containing verses and numbers from al-Qur'an, constructed by Shaykhs for healing purposes.

Ta'wil: Allegorical exegesis for al-Qur'an.

Tab': Nature.

Taba: Another name for Medina.

Tabi'a al-Jamiyya: 'The totalizing nature' of the Prophet (SAW).

Tabib: Physician.

Tabligh: 'Propagating the message,' quality of a prophet.

Tadbir: Self-direction, self-willing.

Tadmin: Inclusion.

Tafsir: Literally, explaining. Commentary and exposition of al-Qur'an.

Tahajjud: Night optional prayers offered at any time after Isha and before Fajr.

Tahara: Ritual purity. (See also: Wudu; Tayammum).

Tahir: Pure.

Taj: 'Crown.' Dervish cap.

Tajahul al-Arif: Feigned ignorance.

Tajalli: Manifestation; illumination witnessed by the inner eye of the seeker.

Tajdid: Renewal.

Tajrid: Outwardly the abandonment of the desires of this world. Inwardly the rejection of compensation and expectation of reward in this world or the next. Isolation.

Takbir: Saying 'Allahu Akbar!' (God is Greatest).

Takbira: A single utterance of 'Allahu Akbar!.'

Taklif: The obligation of a human being to choose the service of God; A constituting principle of this world according to Ibn Arabi.

Talab al-Hadith: Traveling in search of *Hadith*.

Talbiya: Saying 'Labbaik Allahumma Labbaik' (O Allah, I am obedient to your orders, I respond to your call; or: Here I am God, here I am).

Talib ad-Dunya: 'Who seeks the world.'

Talib al-Akhira: 'Who seeks the Otherworld.'

Talib al-Maula: 'Who seeks the Lord.'

Talqin: Recitation of the Shahada in a dying person's ear.

Talqin ad-Dhikr: Teaching the Dhikr.

Tanazzul: Descent or re-descent from the Divine Reality.

Tannur: (Alchemical) Oven.

Tapas: Ascetic heat.

Taqlid: Imitation.

Taqrir: Silent approval.

Taqwa: Being careful. Knowing one's place in the Cosmos. Its proof is the experience of awe.

Tarannum: Recitation.

Tarawih: Optional prayers offered after the Isha prayer on the nights of Ramadan.

Taraqqin: Ascent or ascension.

Tariq: Path.

Tariqat: The Sufi path; a stage of development in Sufism.

Tark at-Tark: 'Quit quitting,' complete surrender.

Tasarruf: Power of the shaykh to bring about events.

Tasawwuf: The Islamic Mystic Path which contains knowledge leading to purification of the human soul. Commonly referred to as Sufism.

Tasbih: Glorification. A string of beads used to count the Names of God, remembrances of Him, His due praises and glorifications. A rosary.

Tasdiq: Faith.

Tashahud: 'I testify that none has the right to be worshiped except Allah, and that Muhammad is his Apostle.

Tashmit: 'May Allah bestow His blessings upon you.'

Taslimiyyet: Submission to God. In Sufism, deep surrender and total submission to God after long-standing pain, resistance, and struggle with oneself.

Tasliya: The formula of blessing upon the Prophet (SAW) (see also: (SAW)).

Tauba: (or *Tawwab*, etc.) 'The Acceptor of Repentance,' a name of God. Repentance. Turning to face the Real whereas before one turned one's back.

Tawaf: The circumambulation of the Kaaba.

Tawajjuh: Strong concentration of master and disciple on each other.

Tawajud: Trying to reach ecstasy.

Tawakkal-Allah: Absolute trust and surrender; handing over responsibility for everything to God.

Tawakkul: Trust in God.

Tawali': Ascendant stars. These are the lights of Tawheed overpowering all lesser lights.

Tawheed: (or *Tawhid*, etc.) Is of three kinds:

  1. *Tawheed al-Rububiya*: Unity of Lordship.

  2. *Tawheed al-Uloohiya*: Unity of Worship.

  3. *Tawheed al-Asma was-Sifat*: Unity of the Names and qualities of God. All three are included in the statement: 'None has the right to be worshiped but God.' The absolute unity of God expressed in the phrase 'La ilaha ila 'llah'— 'There is no God but God.' Monotheism. (See also: Tashahud, Shirk).

Tawheed Al-Itaba: The Unity of following Allah's Apostle Muhammad, included in the meaning of: 'I testify that Muhammad is God's Apostle.'

Tayammum: A form of purification of the body for prayer when water is not available for ablution.

Tayy al-Makan: To change one's place, ubiquity.

Tekiya: A 'corner.' A building established by the Shaykh for instruction and training of murids and dervishes.

Tekke: A dervish lodge. (See also: Tekiya).

Tennure: White sleeveless frock of the Mevlevi order.

Terceman: Turkish prayer in the Bektashi order.

Tibb an-Nabawi: 'Prophetic medicine.'

Timthal: Effigy.

Tiru Qur'an: The Original Qur'an; the Inner Qur'an inscribed within the heart.

Tughra: Hand sign of a ruler. Twisted calligraphic form.

Tul al-Amal: Extended hope.

Tulaqa: Those persons who embraced Islam on the day of the conquest of Mecca.

Tunukzarfi: The quality of too shallow a vessel.

Turbe: A tomb.

U

'Ubudiyya: The quality of the servant, said to be perfected in Muhammad (SAW).

Uflemek: 'Breathing' on someone for healing purposes.

'Ulama: (sing. 'Alim) Men of outward knowledge.

Ulema: The lawyer divines and theologians.

Ulul-'Azm: 'Those with firm intention.' (Sura 46:34).

Umm Abiha: 'Her father's mother,' an epithet of Fatima.

Umm al-Kitab: 'The Mother of the Book,' the heavenly prototype of al-Qur'an.

Ummat: (or *Umma*) Community or nation.

Ummi: Illiterate, 'unlettered,' the state of the Prophet (SAW) in which he was a pure vessel for the Divine revelation of al-Qur'an.

Ummul-Qur'an: The 'source' or 'mother' of al-Qur'an, used commonly to refer to the opening chapter, the Suratul-Fatihah. It is said that within the 124 letters of this Sura is contained the meaning of the entire Qur'an.

Umra: A religious journey to Mecca in which one performs the Tawaf around the Kaaba and the Sa'i ('the going,' the part of the regular Hajj, between the mountains of Safa and Marwa). The Lesser Pilgrimage.

Unio Mystica: Mystical union on various symbolic levels.

Uns: Intimacy.

Uqlat al-Mustawfiz: 'The spell of the Obedient Servant,' a book by Ibn Arabi on the Complete Man.

Uqtuluni: 'Kill me,' the beginning of Hallaj's most famous long poem.

'Uqul: (sing. 'Aql) 'Intelligences.'

Urs: 'Wedding,' celebrations during a saint's death anniversary. Rumi anticipated his death as completed unity in God; his 'wedding day' with his Beloved.

Usedh: Master, teacher, professor.

Ustadh: A name for a Sufi master or other learned teacher.

Uswa Hasana: 'A Beautiful Example,' is Muhammad (SAW) for his community.

Uwaisi: A mystic who has entered the mystical path without formal initiation by a living master. Term refers to Uways al-Qarani, who never physically met the Prophet (SAW), yet because of his piety was known to Muhammad (SAW) who said, referring to Uways: 'The breath of the Merciful (Nafas ar-Rahman) comes to me from Yemen.'

V

Vilayetname: 'Book of sainthood,' hagiographical works.

W

Wa'd-Duha: 'By the Morning Light,' beginning of Sura 93, applied to the Prophet's radiant beauty.

Wa Rahmatullahi Wa Barakatuhu: And the mercy of Allah and His blessings.

Wadad: 'Love, loving friendship.'

Wadud: 'The Loving,' a name of God.

Wahdaniyya: Divine Unity.

Wahdat al-Wujud: 'Unity of Being.'

Wahdat ash-Shuhud: Contemplation, witnessing.

Wahm: Imagination; the power of conceiving what is not present; the decision of Allah.

Wahshat: Loneliness; estrangement.

Waiahaka: May Allah be merciful to you.

Wajd: 'Finding' ecstacy.

Wakeel: A guardian. Usually chief subordinate of a Shaykh.

Wali: (pl. *Awliya*) The 'friend' of Allah, referring to his station of knowledge of the Real by direct seeing. The Saint.

Wali Allah: An equivalent to 'Ali.

Wali Minnat Allah: Saint through love.

Wali Sidq Allah: Saint through works.

Waqf: (pl. *Wasq*) Religious endowment. Also: a pause for breath marked in a written copy of al- Qur'an.

Waqfa: 'Standing.'

Waqif: One who stops. The seeker who reaches his object remains in contemplation or returns to the world.

Waqt: Moment; in Sufism, the duration of an episode of real conscious existence, of remembrance of God. The 'now' that reflects Eternity.

Wara: Abstinence.

Warid: (pl. *Waridat*) That which descends on the awareness of one performing Dhikr or sitting with a teacher. It is the first stage of awakening.

Wasala: To be united, to have arrived at unity.

Wasiya: Testament, last will, exhortation.

Watan: Homeland, from the same root as Mawatin, Realm.

Wazir: 'A helper.'

Wilayat: (or *Vilayat*) God's ultimate, all-encompassing Power. Sanctity.

Wine: al-Qohol. Intoxicating substance used both literally (forbidden in exoteric Islam) and figuratively (in poetry, describing ecstatic states, etc.).

Wird: A unit of Dhikr constructed to contain it in certain patterns of knowledge and self-awakening.

Wisal: Fasting for more than one day continuously. Also: Union; wedding; unity.

Witr: An odd number (1, 3, etc.) of Rak'at with which one finishes one's prayers at night after Isha prayer.

Wudd: 'Love, charity.'

Wujud: An existence, usually of the kinds:

1. *Wajibul Wujud*: A necessary existence, referring to Allah.

2. *Mumkinul Wujud*: a possible existence, referring to the manifest creation.

3. *Mumtainul Wujud*: an impossible existence, referring to an association to God.

Y

Ya: A form of address, as an 'O' so and so. A title of praise, of greatness and glory.

Ya Hayyu! Ya Qayyam!: Literally, 'O the living! O the Everlasting!' According to some sufis, these two attributes together comprise the greatest Name of Allah.

Yad Dasht: Concentration upon God, in Naqshbandi theory.

Yad Kard: Recollection, in Naqshbandi theory.

Yaqin: Certainty. Perfect, absolute faith.

Yaquta Baida: White chrysolite.

Yar-i Ghar: 'The friend of the cave,' Abu Bakr as the closest friend of Muhammad (SAW).

Yasin: Title of Sura 36, also a name of the Prophet (SAW).

Yathrib: A name of Medina.

Yatim: Orphan.

Yatima: 'Orphan (ie. unique) pearl.'

Yawm al-Qiyamah: The Day of Judgment.

Z

Zaboor: Hinduism.

Zahid: (pl. *Zuhhad*) Ascetic, or one who renounces the world.

Zahid-i Zahirparast: The ascetic who is still interested in outward things.

Zahir: The Outwardly manifest, the Evident.

Zahma: Pain.

Zakat: The wealth tax obligatory on Muslims each year, reckoned at 2.5%. Literally: 'Purification.'

Zalim: Tyrant, who loves God for his own sake, Nafs.

Zalimeen: Wrongdoers, sometimes people who wrong themselves; people of darkness, oppressors.

Zamzam: The sacred well inside the Haram (Great Mosque) in Mecca.

Zanadaqa: A body of dualistic or heretical beliefs.

Zanadiqa: Atheists.

Zat: The essence of God; His treasury; His wealth of Purity. His grace.

Zawaya: Berber North African religious lineages.

Zawiyya: Literally, a corner. The building used as a meeting place by the shaykhs of instruction. (See also *Tekiya*, *Khaniqah*).

Zia: Ray of sun.

Zindiq: Heretic.

Zirayat: A visit of a tomb or sacred place.

Zuhd: Renunciation.

Zuhdiyyat: Ascetic verse.

Zuhr: Noon. The mid-day prayer is called Zuhr prayer.

Zuhurat: Obvious, external, perceptible. (See also: Zahir).

Zulf: 'Tresses.'

Zulfikar: Name of a celebrated sword given by Prophet Muhammad (SAW) to Hazreti Ali.

BIBLIOGRAPHY

Addas, Claude. *Quest for the Red Sulphur: The Life of Ibn 'Arabi*. Cambridge: Islamic Texts Society, 1993.

Affifi, A.E. *The Mystical Philosophy of Muhyid Din Ibnul Arabi*. Cambridge: Cambridge University Press, 1979.

Agrippa, Henricus Cornelius. *De occulta philosophia*. Graz: Akad. Druck- und Verlagsanstalt, 1967.

Albertus, Frater. *Alchemist's Handbook*. Weiser. York Beach, 1974.

al-Bukhari, Muhammad Ibn Ismail Ibn al-Mughirah. *Sahih al-Bukhari*. Nine vols. Trans. by Dr. Muhammad Muhsin Khan. Beirut: Dar al-Arabia.

al-Ghazzali, Abu Hamid. *The Alchemy of Happiness*. Trans. by Claud Field. London: Octagon, 1980.

al-Hallaj, Mansur. *The Tawasin*. London: Diwan, 1974.

Allen, Paul M. (ed.) *A Christian Rosenkreutz Anthology*. Blauvelt, NY: Rudolf Steiner Publications, 1968.

Andrae, Tor. *In the Garden of Myrtles*. Albany: SUNY Press, 1987.

'Arabi, Ibn Muhyiddin. *Al-Durrat al-fakhirah*. Trans. by R.J.W. Austin. London: George Allen and Unwin, Ltd., 1970.

———. *Fusus al-Hikam*. Titus Burckhardt, trans. Aldsworth: Beshara Publications, 1975.

———. *Journal of the Muhyiddin Ibn 'Arabi Society*. Vols. I–XV. Oxford, 1982–1994.

———. *Lubbu-L-Lubb*. Ismail Hakki Bursevi, trans. Sherborne: Beshara Publications, n.d.

———. *Ruh al-quds*. Trans. by R.J.W. Austin. London: George Allen & Unwin, Ltd., 1970.

Arnold, Sir Thomas W. *Painting in Islam: A Study of the Place of Pictorial Art in Muslim Culture*. New York: Dover, 1965.

Asad, Muhammad. *This Law of Ours*. Gibraltar: Dar al-Andalus, 1987.

'Ata'Illah, Ibn. *Kitab al-Hikam*. Victor Danner, trans. New York: Paulist Press, 1978.

Attar, Farid al-Din. *Tadhkirat al-Auliya*. A.J. Arberry, trans. New York: Viking Press, 1990.

Binyon, Laurence, et. al. *Persian Miniature Painting*. New York: Dover, 1971.

Blake, William. *The Marriage of Heaven and Hell*. London: Oxford University Press, 1975.

Burckhardt, Titus. *Alchemy*. London: Stuart & Watkins, 1967.

———. *An Introduction to Sufi Doctrine*. Lahore: Ashraf, 1991.

———. *Mirror of the Intellect: Essays on Traditional Science and Sacred Art*. Albany: SUNY Press, 1987.

———. *Mystical Astrology According to Ibn 'Arabi*. Abingdon: Beshara Publications, 1987.

———. *Sacred Art in East and West: Principles and Methods*. Middlesex: Perennial Books, 1977.

Chishti, Hakim, G.M. *The Traditional Healer's Handbook: A Classic Guide to the Medicine of Avicenna*. Rochester: Healing Arts Press, 1988.

Chishti, Shaykh Hakim Moinuddin. *The Book of Sufi Healing*. Rochester: Inner Traditions, 1991.

Chittick, William. *The Sufi Path of Knowledge*. Albany: SUNY Press, 1989.

———. *Imaginal Worlds: Ibn al-'Arabi and the Problem of Religious Diversity*. Albany: SUNY Press, 1994.

Chodkiewicz, Michel. *An Ocean Without Shore: Ibn Arabi, The Book, and the Law*. Albany: SUNY Press, 1993.

Cleary, Thomas. *The Wisdom of the Prophet*. Boston: Shambala, 1994.

Cook, Roger. *The Tree of Life: Image for the Cosmos*. New York: Thames and Hudson, 1974.

Corbin, Henri. *Avicenna and the Visionary Recital*. Princeton: Princeton University Press, 1988.

———. *Creative Imagination in the Sufism of Ibn 'Arabi*. Princeton: Princeton University Press, 1969.

———. *Cyclical Time and Ismaili Gnosis*. London: Kegan Paul, 1983.

———. *Spiritual Body and Celestial Earth: From Mazdean Iran to Shi'ite Iran*. Princeton: Princeton University Press, 1977.

Dehlvi (Rah), Seh banul Hind Hazrat Maulana Ahmed Saeed. *Hadees-E-Qudsi*. Trans. by Mohd. Hanif Khan. Delhi: Dini Book Depot, 1990.

De Lubicz, R.A. Schwaller. *Nature Word*. Trans. by Deborah Lawlor. West Stockbridge, MA: Lindisfarne, 1982.

Evola, Julius. *The Hermetic Tradition*. Rochester: Inner Traditions, 1994.

(Fulcanelli). *Fulcanelli Master Alchemist: Esoteric Interpretations of the Hermetic Symbols of the Great Work. A Translation of Fulcanelli's Le Mystere des Cathedrales* by Mary Sworder. Albuquerque: Brotherhood of Life, 1984.

Hayyan, Jabir Ibn. *Of Furnaces*. Edmonds, WA: The Alchemical Press, 1984.

————. *Book of the Invention of Verity*. Edmonds, WA: The Alchemical Press, 1989.

————. *The Discovery of Secrets*. Trans. by Robert R. Steele. Edmonds, WA: The Alchemical Press, 1988.

————. Lory, Pierre. *Dix Traites d'alchimie*. Paris: Islam Sinbad, 1983.

————. Russell, Richard, trans. *The Alchemical Works of Geber*. York Beach, ME: Weiser, 1994.

Junius, Manfred M. *The Practical Handbook of Plant Alchemy*. Rochester: Healing Arts Press, 1993.

Hirtenstein, S. and Tiernan, M., eds. *Muhyiddin Ibn 'Arabi: A Commemorative Volume*. Rockport, ME: Element, 1993.

'Iraqi, Fakhruddin. *Divine Flashes. (Lama'at)*. William C. Chittick and Peter Lamborn Wilson, trans. New York: Paulist Press, 1982.

————. *The Book of Knowledge Acquired Concerning the Cultivation of Gold: An Arabic Alchemical Treatise*. Trans. by E.J. Holmyard. Edmonds, WA: The Alchemical Press, 1991.

Keynes, Sir Godffrey. *Drawings of William Blake: 92 Pencil Studies*. New York: Dover, 1970.

Maier, Michael. *Atalanta Fugiens: An Edition of the Emblems, Fugues, and Epigrams*. Trans. by Joscelyn Godwin. Grand Rapids, MI: Phanes, 1989.

Massignon, Louis. *The Passion of al-Hallaj*. 4 vols. Trans. by Herbert Mason. Princeton: Princeton University Press, 1982.

Meherally, Akbarally. *A History of the Agakhani Ismailis*. Burnaby: A.M. Trust, 1991.

————. *Understanding Ismailism*, A Unique Tariqah of Islam. Burnaby: A.M. Trust, 1988.

Nasr, S.H. *Sufi Essays*. Albany: SUNY Press, 1972.

————. *Three Muslim Sages*. Delmar: Caravan, 1976.

Nurbakhsh, Javad. *Masters of the Path: A History of the Masters of the Nimatullahi Sufi Order*. New York: Khaniqahi-Nimatullahi, 1980.

————. *Sufi Symbolism, vols.* 1–12. New York: Khaniqahi-Nimatullahi, 1986–1995.

————. *The Truths of Love*. New York: Khaniqahi-Nimatullahi, 1982.

Nwyia, Paul. *Exegese coranique et langage mystique*. Beirut, 1970.

Pernety, Antoine-Joseph. *An Alchemical Treatise on the Great Art*. York Beach, ME: Weiser, 1995.

Philalethes, Eirenaeus. *An Open Entrance to the Closed Palace of the King*. Edmonds, WA: Alchemical Press, 1984.

The Holy Qur'an, (Arabic) Text, Translation, and Commentary by Abdullah Yusuf Ali. Elmhurst: Tahrike Tarsile, 1988.

————. *The Koran Interpreted*. Trans. by A.J. Arberry. New York: Collier, 1955.

————. *The Koran*. Trans. by N.J. Dawood. New York: Penguin, 1956.

————. *The Koran*. Trans. by George Sale. New York: American Book Exchange, 1880.

————. *The Meaning of the Glorious Koran*. Trans. by Mohammad Marmaduke Pickthall. New York: Penguin, 1969.

————. *Part Thirty of the Holy Qur'an: Arabic, Translation, and Transliteration*. Ibrahim El Dosougi Mohummad, 1979.

————. *The Qur'an: Shaykh Tabarsi's Commentary*. Trans. by Musa O.A. Abdul. S.H. Lahore: Muhammad Ashraf, 1977.

Rumi, Jalalu'ddin. *The Mathnawi of Jalalu'ddin Rumi*. 3 *vols.* Trans. by Reynold A. Nicholson. Cambridge: E.J.W. Gibb Memorial Trust, 1923.

Schimmel, Annemarie. *As Through a Veil: Mystical Poetry in Islam*. New York: Columbia University Press, 1982.

————. *The Mystery of Numbers*. Oxford: Oxford University Press, 1993.

SUFI: The Magazine of Khaniqahi-Nimatullahi. Issues 1–25. London, 1988–1995.

Suhrawardi, al-Maqtul. *The Mystical and Visionary Treatises of Suhrawardi*. Trans. by W.M. Thackson, Jr. London: Octagon, 1982.

Valentine, Basil. *The Triumphal Chariot of Antimony*. London: James Elliot, 1893.

Vaughn, Thomas. *The Works of Thomas Vaughn Mystic & Alchemist*. Ed. by A.E. Waite. New York: University Books, 1968.

Waite, A.E. *The Alchemical Writings of Edward Kelly*. York Beach, ME: Weiser, 1973.

————. *The Hermetic and Alchemical Writings of Aureolus Philippus Theophrastus Bombast of Hohenheim, Called Paracelsus the Great*. Boston: Shambala, 1976.

————. *The Hermetic Museum*. York Beach, ME: Weiser, 1991.

www.ingramcontent.com/pod-product-compliance
Lightning Source LLC
Chambersburg PA
CBHW031856090426
42741CB00005B/512